DURGA PUJA,LAKSHMI PUJA,SARASWATI PUJA,NAVRATRI PUJA :HINDU HOME PUJA BOOK

Complete Ritual Worship Procedure

Santhi Sivakumar

Credits
Mantra Consultants : Shri Krishna Bhat, Shivakumar
Cover Design : Oxygen Media,canva
Cover Photo : souvik laha,Unsplash
Book Design : Oxygen Media
Photos :Wikimedia,Manaveer-Pixabay, Khirod Behera - Pexels , Tarikul Raana- Unsplash

Asato ma sad-gamaya;
tamaso ma jyotir-gamaya;
mrtyor-ma amrutam gamaya.
Aum. Shanti, shanti shanti

Om. Lead me from unreal to real; lead me from darkness to light; lead me from death to immortality. Om peace, peace, peace

BRIHADARANYAKA UPANISHAD

CONTENTS

SWAGATHAM

Namaste,

Puja or pooja is a ritual worship per formed by Hindus. Puja is showing piety towards the Divine, executed to keep us in agreement with enormous powers, con sequently eliminating and defeating the distresses of life by bringing profound upliftment. While doing puja, consider ations and vibrations of powers are made around us. These powers work to kill the negative impacts throughout our life by encompassing positive energy by which we can have genuine feelings of serenity, material success and empower us to con nect with the Divine.

During a Puja, we often repeat 'sacred mantras' or 'verses' or 'stothras' that help us connect with God to make our mind peaceful. It is believed that wor shiping Deity and regularly doing puja properly will remove all kinds of sor rows and pain.

Beyond our perception and time, Sanskrit is an ancient language and still re maining as reality without any changes and structural modification. The mantras in Sanskrit endowed with powerful vibra tions which our nervous system provide positive energy this is the Power of Man tra Chanting.

On special occasions if you can perform home Pujas by following proper proced ures, It's not only memorable but also auspicious.

I have put in a lot of effort and made many revisions to improve and compile this book. NowI'm happy to pub lish this 'Home Puja Book' consisting of Durgapuja, Lakshmi Puja ,Saraswathi Puja and Navrathiri Puja '. Your valuable sug gestion for improvement is Welcome.

Thanking You.

Santhi Sivakumar

PUJA ESSENTIALS

- Deity (God /Goddess) idol or picture

Puja Utensils

- Puja Lamp with oil or Ghee soaked Cotton Wicks
- Puja Bell
- Coppor Pot or Silver Pot or Stainless steel Vessel (Kalasha)
- Coppor or silver or metal Spoon
- Arati plate
- Small Cups
- Any Jewelry (a bangle or chain for use during the puja)

Basic Puja Materials/Items

- Kumkum(a), Vibhoothi(Holy ash),Turmeric and cups to hold them
- Sandalwood or Sandalpaste
- Akshta - Uncooked Rice mixed with turmeric (using water) in a cup
- Incense sticks
- Champhor (Karpoor)
- Holy Water (Like Ganga Water) or fresh pure water (To be filled in Kalash)
- Rose Water
- Fresh Cloth
- Fresh mango leaves, wash them before using Kalash

- Fresh Flowers to offer Deity
- Match Box
- Puja Manta Book

Other Puja Necessaries

- Coconut
- Paan (betal Leaves) with Supari (If available)
- Fruits
- Sweets
- Banna Leaf (To Offer All Prasad)
- Grass
- Neivedhya Prasada (Fresh Cooked Food)

(Note: Even if you don't have some of the above mentioned items, don't worry! Pray whole heartedly, chant the mantras properly you will get the God/Goddess blessings)

***

STEP BY STEP BASICS TO DO PUJA OR WORSHIP

- ✓ Without taking Bath don't do any puja arrangements
- ✓ Sit on a piece of cloth or mat facing North or East.
- ✓ First, you'll clean the place and idols (*abhisekha: Water is offered for symbolic bathing*) by sprinkling few drops of water.
- ✓ **Vastra** : ("clothing"): Cloth may be wrapped around the image affixed to it
- ✓ **Aabaran:** The deity is decorated with ornaments
- ✓ Light the lamps and ensure that you are placing two lamps (Deepa) on both side (facing east -towards sun or another facing North- for a god).
- ✓ Light an incense stick.
- ✓ Light an small brass oil lamp in keep it on your arati plate. (Use sesame oil ,ghee or mustard oil).
- ✓ **Pushpa** : Offer flowers to God's idols or images. (One flower will also be sufficient)
- ✓ Do Salutation (Namaskar) with folded hands

and closed eyes.

- ✓ Sit down for a minute or two to relax.
- ✓ Start Chanting Sacred Mantras
- ✓ Offer Naivedya Foods such as cooked rice, fruit, Dry grapes,sugar, and betel leaf are offered
- ✓ Puja should be always performed by facing towards East or North
- ✓ After completion of the puja or Dipa(aarti,) make three Circumambulation (parikrama/ Pradakshina) around the deity.
- ✓ Namaskara or pranama. The worshipper and family bow or prostrate themselves before the image to offer homage.
- ✓ Taking leave from Puja

Mantra/ Japa is best done using a strand of beaded mala known as Japa mala made of Rudraksha, red sandal, Tulsi or sphatik beads.

Remember the Following

Tulsi (Basil leaves) should not be offered to Lord Ganesha, Shiva, and Bhairava.

Goddess Durga should not be offered durva grass. This is especially recommended for Ganesha.

Holywater(for kalash) should not be kept in any plastic, aluminum or iron vessels.

You should never face your back towards the idols of Gods and Goddesses.

Dont keep the flowers in hand and offer it to God. Place flowers on a plate and offer it with your fingers.

Dont store sandle paste(chandan) in copper utensils.

***

MANTRA CHANTING RULES

- ✓ Read and pronounce Mantra carefully before starting chant.
- ✓ Do not give a break or end to the process once you have started it.
- ✓ Chanting the mantra out loud or follow Upamsu Japa (The Upamsu Japa : whispering or humming if Mantra which cannot be heard by any one.
- ✓ Chanting should be done with a fixed posture to allow the complete effect of the sound energy.
- ✓ Chanting should not be done like singing, or like reading. It should not be muttered fast, each syllable should be properly uttered with the required stress and pronounced with clarity.
- ✓ Japa - the mantra should be chanted for the count.
- ✓ Avoid activities like sneezing, yawning or spitting (as it shows disrespect or insult of God)

***

BOOK :1 MAA DURGA PUJA

LIST OF POWERFUL SACRED MANTRAS FOR MAA DURGA PUJA (INDEX)

- ***Durga Invocation Mantra***
- ***Durga Moola Mantra*** – *Seed/Root Mantra*
- ***Durga Maha Mantra***
- ***Durga Mantra***
- ***Devi Stuti***
- ***Maa Durga-Duh-Swapna-Nivaaran Mantra :*** *Protection from bad dreams and omens*
- ***Durga Shatru-Shanti Mantra:*** *For destruction of enemies*
- ***Seven Powerful mantras of Maa Durga that solve all your problems***
  1. *Mantra For Removal of all Obstacles (Sarv-Baadha-Mukti Mantra*
  2. *Mantra for wealth*
  3. *Mantra for conquering troubles*
  4. *Mantra for getting power (Shakti)*
  5. *Mantra for good health and fortune*
  6. *Mantra for overcoming fear*
  7. *Mantra for the destruction of a pandemic*
- ***Stotram :*** *Sri Mahiśhāsura Mardinī Stotram*
- ***Namavali :*** *Durgā Aśhṭottara Sata Nāmāvaḻi*
- ***Prayer Mantra (Prarthna)***

***

GODDESS DURGA

The name "**Durga**" signifies 'the invincible' (powerful and unbeatable) in Sanskrit. Goddess Durga is estabilished a main and popular form of the Hindu Goddess Parvati Devi(Wife of Shiva). She's bestowed as "shakti", or the female rule of divine energy. Durga is the other half of Shiva,he is the form and she is the expression (ShivaShakthi). Durga is considered to be the mother (Mātā) of the universe, while Shiva is the father (Pitāḥ). The trinity of Brahma, Vishnu and Shiva came together to create a powerful female form with ten arms to combat the evil demon Mahishasura (buffalo head demon-).Maa Shakthi (Durga)is the goddess of power and strength, is perhaps the most important goddess of the Hindus. Doing the Durga Puja to cure disease helps you to retain good health, encourage prosperity & remove ailments.

Puja and Festival Celebration dedicated to Maa Durga

- Uma Maheshwar Vrata : one of the holy astha maha vartams that are mentioned in the Skandha Puraan.
- Gowri Vratha ; usually doing by married women on each Tuesday in Shravana month
- *Gowri* Habba : a day before Ganesh Chaturthi
- SampathGowri Vratha : every Friday for a year or on a Full moon day on Vaishaka Month
- Navrathiri (First, second and third days of Navaratri)
- Vijayadasami (Last day of Navarathiri)
- All Tuesdays and Fridays

(Note: Please check and verify exact dates of festival celebrations in Hindu calendars or Panchang)

***

MAA DURGA PUJA MANTRAS

"Surrender all actions and obligations onto me and I shall release thee from all fears".

Invocation to Lord Ganesh

Vakra-Tunndda Maha-Kaaya Suurya-Kotti Samaprabha |
Nirvighnam Kuru Me Deva Sarva-Kaaryessu Sarvadaa ||

वक्रतुण्ड महाकाय सूर्यकोटि समप्रभ ।
निर्विघ्नं कुरु मे देव सर्वकार्येषु सर्वदा ॥

Salutations to Sri Ganesha : O Lord, Who has a Curved Trunk, Who has a Large Body, Whose aura is like light of crores of sun, Please make my entire work obstacle free, forever.

Chanting of this mantra helps to achieve wealth, wisdom, good luck, prosperity and success in all the endeavors.

Shanthi Mantra

Om Saha Naav (au)-Avatu |
Saha Nau Bhunaktu |
Saha Viiryam Karavaavahai |
Tejasvi Naav[au]Adhii tam-Astu Maa Vidvissaavahai |

Om Shaantih: Shaantih: Shaantih: ||

ॐ सह नाववतु ।
सह नौ भुनक्तु ।
सह वीर्यं करवावहै ।
तेजस्वि नावधीतमस्तु मा विद्विषावहै ।
ॐ शान्तिः शान्तिः शान्तिः ॥

Om, May He protect us both together; may He nourish us both togethe.Together may we perform . May what has been Studied by us be vigorous and effective; .Om! Let there be peace in me! May peace be unto us, and may peace be unto all living beings.

This Shanti mantra, prayer for peace found in the krishna Yajurveda Taittiriya Upanishad (2.2.2).This mantra purifies the body and relieves it from the sufferings, diseases and discomforts.

Asana Puja

Om Prthvi Tvayaa Dhrtaa Lokaa Devi Tvam Vissnnunaa Dhrtaa | Tvam Ca Dhaaraya Maam Devi Pavitram Kuru Ca-[A]asanam ||

ॐ पृथ्वि त्वया धृता लोका
देवि त्वं विष्णुना धृता ।
त्वं च धारय मां देवि
पवित्रं कुरु चासनम् ॥

Om, O Prithivi Devi /Bhoomi Devi, You are borne the entire world Please hold me O Devi, and make this seat of the worshipper Pure.

Deepa Puja

Shubham Karoti Kalyaannam-Aarogyam Dhana-Sampadaa |
Shatru-Buddhi-Vinaashaaya Diipa-Jyotir-Namostute ||

शुभं करोति कल्याणमारोग्यं धनसंपदा ।
शत्रुबुद्धिविनाशाय दीपज्योतिर्नमोऽस्तुते ॥

Salutations to the Light of the Lamp, Which Brings Auspiciousness, Health and Prosperity; Which Destroys Inimical Feelings

Gayatri Mantra for Pranayama

Om Bhuuh : Om Bhuvah: Om Svah: Om Mahah :Om Janah : Om Tapah: Om Satyam
Om Tat-Savitur Varennyam Bhargo Devasya Dhiimahi
Dhiyo Yo Nah Pracodayaat |
Om Aapo Jyotii Rasoa Amrtam Brahma Bhuur Bhuvah: SvarOm ||

(Touch the ears three times and saying Om, Om , Om)

ॐ भूः ॐ भुवः ॐ स्वः
ॐ महः ॐ जनः ॐ तपः ॐ सत्यम्
ॐ तत्सवितुर्वरेण्यं भर्गो देवस्य धीमहि
धियो यो नः प्रचोदयात् ।
ॐ आपो ज्योती रसोऽमृतं ब्रह्म भूर्भुवः स्वरोम् ॥

Yajur Veda: Taittiriya Aranyaka

Om,I meditate on the Consciousness of the Physical Plane, Om, I meditate on the intercede Space, Om, I meditate on the Heaven, Consciousness of the beginning of the Divine Mind.(the meditation goes to subtler levels)

This strengthens our mind with concentration and gives immense peace to us.

SANKALPA MANTRA

For Saivas :

Mamo partha samastha duritha kshaya dwara ,

Sri Parameshwara preethyartham

Sri Parvathi prasada sidhyartham

Asmaham Sakudumbanam

shemasya, dhairyasya, dhairya, vijaya, ayur, arogya, ishwarya, abhivrithyartham, Kalyana Prapyartham, Sakala vasikaranartham

Mahaganaptim pujam karishye

For Vaishnavas:

Mamo partha samastha duritha kshaya dwara ,

Sri Narayana Preethyartham

Sri Parvathi prasada sidhyartham

Asmaham Sakudumbanam

shemasya, dhairyasya, dhairya, vijaya, ayur, arogya, ishwarya, abhivrithyartham, Kalyana Prapyartham, Sakala vasikaranartham

Mahaganaptim pujam karishye

Om For removing all problems and pains in life.For making Lord happy. For blessings of Goddess Parvathi. For getting my above wishes fulfilled.

The procedure of making a decision to perform the pooja for the welfare of all concerned.

Kalash(a) Puja

Kalashasya mukhe Vishnu: kanTe rudrassamaasrita:|
Mule tatra sthitho brahma madhye matrugana: smruta: ||
kukshou thu saagara: sarve sapthadveepa vasundhara: |
Rigvedoatha yajurveda: saama vedo atharvavana: ||
angaischa sahita ssarve kalashaambu samaasrita: |

कलशस्य मुखे विष्णु: कण्ठे रुद्र: समाश्रित:|
मूले तस्य स्थितो ब्रह्मा मध्ये मातृगणा: स्थिता ||
कुक्षौ तु सागर: सर्वे सप्तद्वीपा वसुन्धरा |

ऋग्वेदो यजुर्वेदः सामवेदो अथर्वणः ||
अङ्गैश्च सहितं सर्वे कलशाम्बु समाश्रिताः |

Kalash(a) is traditionally a copper pot. Fill it up with water and put two or three leaves of tulsi leaves or flower petals as well . Take few more couple of flower petals (or Tulsi leaves) dip it in the pot water and sprinkle it around the area you are seated . Then sprinkle the few drops of water if,other people seated around you .

Invite all the holy rivers like Ganga,yamuna, saraswati,narmada, godavari, sindhu,kaveri into this water pot . Invite all the gods ie Brahma, Vishnu, Shiva, Ganesh. (May come to me to bestow Peace and remove the Evil Influences)

Ghanta Puja

Aagama Artham Tu Devaanaam Gamana Artham Tu Rakssasaam |
Ghannttaa Ravam Karomya(ia)adau Devataa Ahvaana Laan chanam ||

आगमार्थं तु देवानां गमनार्थं तु रक्षसाम् ।
घण्टारवं करोम्यादौ देवताह्वान लाञ्छनम् ॥

For the purpose of inviting the Divine Forces and removing Evil Forces, I make the (Ghanta) Bell Sound.

Durga Invocation Mantra

ya devi sarvabhutesu visnumayeti

sabdita , namastasyai namastasyai namastasyai namo nam(ah):

या देवी सर्वभूतेषु विष्णुमायेति शब्दिता, नमस्तस्यी नमस्तस्यी नमस्तस्यी नमो नम:

O Devi, the omniscient, We bow to your majesty again and again. Please bless us

(Note: You can chant this mantra 3 or 9 or 18 times to get more benefit)

Durga Moola Mantra

Om Hreeng Dung Durgaayai Nama(h): ||

ॐ ह्रीं दुं दुर्गायै नमः ||

Seed Mantra.Moola mantra as it stands pertains to a particular god or goddess. This is most effective and secret Mantra and has power to fulfill all suitable desires.

(Note: You can chant this mantra 3 or 9 or 18 times to get more benefit)

Durga Maha Mantra

Om Aing Hreeng Kleeng Chamundaayai Viche ||

ॐ ऐं ह्रीं क्लीं चामुण्डायै विच्चे ||

Maha means "great" and mantra definition is "sacred chant for deliverance."

By reciting this Mantra one gets realization of self.

(Note: You can chant this mantra 3 or 9 or 18 times to get more benefit)

Durga Mantra

Sarva Mangala Mangalye Sive Sarvartha Sadhike |
Saranye Trayambike Gauri Narayani Namostute ||

सर्वमङ्गलमाङ्गल्ये शिवे सर्वार्थसाधिके ।
शरण्ये त्र्यम्बके गौरि नारायणि नमोऽस्तु ते ॥

This mantra is chanted almost during all days, all celebrations, all rituals and festivals. Regular chanting can give wisdom and strength combined with a prosperous life. Mantra for welfare.

Devi Stuti

Ya devi sarva bhutesu, shanti rupena sansitha |
ya devi sarva bhutesu, shakti rupena sansthita |
ya devi sarva bhutesu, matra rupena sansthita |
Namastasyai, namastasyai, namastasyai, namo namaha: ||

या देवी सर्वभुतेषु क्षान्तिरूपेण संस्थिता ।
या देवी सर्वभुतेषु शक्तिरूपेण संस्थिता ।
या देवी सर्वभुतेषु मातृरूपेण संस्थिता ।

या देवी सर्वभुतेषु बुद्धिरूपेण संस्थिता ।
नमस्तस्यै नमस्तस्यै नमस्तस्यै नमो नमः ॥

This Mantra blesses one with power, prosperity and positive energy. It helps to build inner power and allows to develop healthy, loving relationships. Chanting of this Mantra blocks negative thoughts and banish ignorance.

Maa Durga-Duh-Swapna-Nivaaran Mantra

Shanti karmani sarvatra tatha duh swapna darshane |
Grah pidaasu chograsu maahaatmyam srinu yaanmam ||

शान्तिकर्मणि सर्वत्र तथा दुःस्वप्नदर्शने |
ग्रहपीडासु चोग्रासु माहात्म्यं श्रृणुयान्मम ||

If one often suffer from nightmares (Bad dreams), chanting this Mantra will help to get relief and protection from bad dreams and omens. Soon you will be free from negative thought.

Durga Shatru-Shanti Mantra

Ripavah sankshayam yaanti kalyaanam chop padyate |
Nandate cha kulam punsaam maahaatmyam mam srinu yaanmam ||

रिपव: संक्षयम् यान्ति कल्याणम चोपपद्यते।
नन्दते च कुलम पुंसाम माहात्म्यम मम श्रृणुयान्मम ||

Chanting this Durga Mantra will help to seek protection against all the negativeness, enemies and adversaries. This Durga Shatru-Shanti Mantra even has the power to destroy our enemies. Recite this mantra can bring balance, prosperity, bliss, and peace in our life

Powerful mantras of Maa Durga that solve all your problems

Mantra For Removal of all Obstacles

Om Sarvabaadhaa Vinirmukto, Dhan Dhaanyah Sutaanvitah |
Manushyo Matprasaaden Bhavishyati Na Sanshayah: Om ||

ॐ सर्वाबाधा विनिर्मुक्तो, धन धान्यः सुतान्वितः।
मनुष्यो मत्प्रसादेन भविष्यति न संशयः ॐ ।।

Mantra for wealth

Durge Smrita Harasi Bhitimshesh jantoh: Swasthaih :Smritamati Mateev Shubhaam Dadasi Daridray Duh:kh Bhayaharini ka Twadanya Sarvopakarkaranay Sadadrachitta ||

दुर्गे स्मृता हरसि भीतिमशेषजन्तो: स्वस्थै: स्मृता मतिमतीव शुभां ददासि।

दारिद्र्यदुःखभयहारिणि का त्वदन्या सर्वोपकारकरणाय सदाऽऽर्द्रचित्ता॥

Mantra for conquering troubles

Sharanagat Deenart Paritranaparayane |

Sarvsyartihare Devi, NarayaniNamostute||

शरणागतदीनार्तपरित्राणपरायणे।
सर्वस्यार्तिहरे देवि नारायणि नमोऽस्तु ते॥

Mantra for getting power (Shakti)

Srishtisthiti Vinashaanam Shaktibhute Sanatani Gunaashraye Gunamaye NarayaniNamostute ||

सृष्टिस्थितिविनाशानां शक्ति भूते सनातनि। गुणाश्रये
गुणमये नारायणि नमोऽस्तु ते॥

Mantra for good health and fortune

Dehi Saubhagyamaarogyam Dehi Me Paramam Sukham Rupam Dehi Jayam Dehi, Yasho Dehi DwikhoJahi ||

देहि सौभाग्यमारोग्यं देहि मे परमं सुखम्। रूपं देहि
जयं देहि यशो देहि द्विषो जहि॥

Mantra for overcoming fear

Sarvaswarupe Sarveshe Sarvashakti Samanvite BhayeBhyastrahi No Devi! Durge DeviNamostute ||

सर्वस्वरूपे सर्वेशे सर्वशक्ति समन्विते। भयेभ्याहि

नो देवि दुर्गे देवि नमोऽस्तु ते॥

Mantra for the destruction of a pandemic

Jayanti Mangala Kali, Bhadrakali Kapalini Durga Kshama Shiva Dhatri Swaha Swadha Namoastute Te||

जयन्ती मङ्गला काली भद्रकाली कपालिनी। दुर्गा क्षमा
शिवा धात्री स्वाहा स्वधा नमोऽस्तु ते॥

(Note: You can chant these mantras 3 or 9 or 18 times to get more benefit)

Sri Mahiśhāsura Mardinī Stotram

"The place where Sri Mahishasura Mardini Stotram is chant every day, I will always be present and never leave."

- Maa Durga's proclamation (Devi Mahatmyam, 12th chapter)

Ayi girinandini nanditamedini viśva-vinodini nandanute
girivara vindhya-śiroadhi-nivāsini viśhṇu-vilāsini jiśhṇunute |
bhagavati he śitikaṇṭha-kuṭumbiṇi bhūrikuṭumbiṇi bhūrikṛte
jaya jaya he mahiśhāsura-mardini ramyakapardini śailasute || 1 ||

अयि गिरिनन्दिनि नन्दितमेदिनि विश्व-विनोदिनि नन्दनुते
गिरिवर विन्ध्य-शिरोऽधि-निवासिनि विष्णु-विलासिनि जिष्णुनुते।

भगवति हे शितिकण्ठ-कुटुम्बिणि भूरिकुटुम्बिणि भूरिकृते
जय जय हे महिषासुर-मर्दिनि रम्यकपर्दिनि शैलसुते || 1 ||

suravara-harśhiṇi durdhara-dharśhiṇi
durmukha-marśhiṇi harśharate
tribhuvana-pośhiṇi śaṅkara-tośhiṇi
kalmaśha-mośhiṇi ghośharate |
danuja-niróśhiṇi ditisuta-rośhiṇi
durmada-śośhiṇi sindhusute
jaya jaya he mahiśhāsura-mardini
ramyakapardini śailasute || 2 ||

सुरवर-हर्षिणि दुर्धर-धर्षिणि दुर्मुख-मर्षिणि हर्षरते
त्रिभुवन-पोषिणि शङ्कर-तोषिणि कल्मष-मोषिणि घोषरते |
दनुज-निरोषिणि दितिसुत-रोषिणि दुर्मद-शोषिणि सिन्धुसुते
जय जय हे महिषासुर-मर्दिनि रम्यकपर्दिनि शैलसुते || 2 ||

ayi jagadamba madamba kadambavana-
priyavāsini hāsarate
śikhari-śiromaṇi tuṅa-himālaya-
śṛṅganijālaya-madhyagate |
madhumadhure madhu-kaitabha-gañjini
kaitabha-bhañjini rāsarate
jaya jaya he mahiśhāsura-mardini
ramyakapardini śailasute || 3 ||

अयि जगदम्ब मदम्ब कदम्बवन-प्रियवासिनि हासरते
शिखरि-शिरोमणि तुङ-हिमालय-शृङ्गनिजालय-मध्यगते |

मधुमधुरे मधु-कैतभ-गञ्जिनि कैतभ-भञ्जिनि रासरते
जय जय हे महिषासुर-मर्दिनि रम्यकपर्दिनि शैलसुते || 3 ||

ayi śatakhaṇḍa-vikhaṇḍita-ruṇḍa-
vituṇḍita-śuṇḍa-gajādhipate
ripu-gaja-gaṇḍa-vidāraṇa-chaṇḍaparāk-
rama-śauṇḍa-mṛgādhipate |
nija-bhujadaṇḍa-nipāṭita-chaṇḍa-
nipāṭita-muṇḍa-bhaṭādhipate
jaya jaya he mahiśhāsura-mardini
ramyakapardini śailasute || 4 ||

अयि शतखण्ड-विखण्डित-रुण्ड-वितुण्डित-शुण्ड-गजाधिपते
रिपु-गज-गण्ड-विदारण-चण्डपराक्रम-शौण्ड-मृगाधिपते |
निज-भुजदण्ड-निपाटित-चण्ड-निपाटित-मुण्ड-भटाधिपते
जय जय हे महिषासुर-मर्दिनि रम्यकपर्दिनि शैलसुते || 4 ||

ayi raṇadurmada-śatru-vadhodita-
durdhara-nirjara-śakti-bhṛte
chatura-vichāra-dhurīṇa-mahāśaya-dūta-
kṛta-pramathādhipate |
durita-durīha-durāśaya-durmati-dānava-
dūta-kṛtāntamate
jaya jaya he mahiśhāsura-mardini
ramyakapardini śailasute || 5 ||

अयि रणदुर्मद-शत्रु-वधोदित-दुर्धर-निर्जर-शक्ति-भृते
चतुर-विचार-धुरीण-महाशय-दूत-कृत-प्रमथाधिपते |
दुरित-दुरीह-दुराशय-दुर्मति-दानव-दूत-कृतान्तमते

जय जय हे महिषासुर-मर्दिनि रम्यकपर्दिनि शैलसुते || 5 ||

ayi nija huṅkṛtimātra-nirākṛta-
dhūmravilochana-dhūmraśate
samara-viśośhita-śoṇitabīja-
samudbhavaśoṇita-bīja-late |
śiva-śiva-śumbhaniśumbha-mahāhava-
tarpita-bhūtapiśācha-pate
jaya jaya he mahiśhāsura-mardini
ramyakapardini śailasute || 6 ||

अयि निज हुङ्कृतिमात्र-निराकृत-धूम्रविलोचन-धूम्रशते
समर-विशोषित-शोणितबीज-समुद्भवशोणित-बीज-लते |
शिव-शिव-शुम्भनिशुम्भ-महाहव-तर्पित-भूतपिशाच-पते
जय जय हे महिषासुर-मर्दिनि रम्यकपर्दिनि शैलसुते || 6 ||

dhanuranusaṅgaraṇa-kśhaṇa-saṅga-
parisphuradaṅga-naṭatkaṭake
kanaka-piśaṅga-pṛśhatka-niśhaṅga-
rasadbhaṭa-śṛṅga-hatāvaṭuke |
kṛta-chaturaṅga-balakśhiti-raṅga-ghaṭad-
bahuraṅga-raṭad-baṭuke
jaya jaya he mahiśhāsura-mardini
ramyakapardini śailasute || 7 ||

धनुरनुसङ्गरण-क्षण-सङ्ग-परिस्फुरदङ्ग-नटत्कटके
कनक-पिशङ्ग-पृषत्क-निषङ्ग-रसद्भट-शृङ्ग-हतावटुके |
कृत-चतुरङ्ग-बलक्षिति-रङ्ग-घटद्-बहुरङ्ग-रटद्-बटुके

जय जय हे महिषासुर-मर्दिनि रम्यकपर्दिनि शैलसुते || 7 ||

ayi śaraṇāgata-vairivadhū-varavīravarā-
bhaya-dāyikare
tribhuvanamastaka-śūla-virodhi-śirodhi-
kṛtā'mala-śūlakare |
dumi-dumi-tāmara-dundubhi-nāda-maho-
mukharīkṛta-diṅnikare
jaya jaya he mahiśhāsura-mardini
ramyakapardini śailasute || 8 ||

अयि शरणागत-वैरिवधू-वरवीरवराभय-दायिकरे
त्रिभुवनमस्तक-शूल-विरोधि-शिरोधि-कृताऽमल-शूलकरे |
दुमि-दुमि-तामर-दुन्दुभि-नाद-महो-मुखरीकृत-दिङ्निकरे
जय जय हे महिषासुर-मर्दिनि रम्यकपर्दिनि शैलसुते || 8 ||

suralalanā-tatatheyi-tatheyi-
tathābhinayodara-nṛtya-rate
hāsavilāsa-hulāsa-mayipraṇa-
tārtajanemita-premabhare |
dhimikiṭa-dhikkaṭa-dhikkaṭa-
dhimidhvani-ghoramṛdaṅga-ninādarate
jaya jaya he mahiśhāsura-mardini
ramyakapardini śailasute || 9 ||

सुरललना-ततथेयि-तथेयि-तथाभिनयोदर-नृत्य-रते
हासविलास-हुलास-मयिप्रण-तार्तजनेमित-प्रेमभरे |
धिमिकिट-धिक्कट-धिक्कट-धिमिध्वनि-घोरमृदङ्ग-निनादरते

जय जय हे महिषासुर-मर्दिनि रम्यकपर्दिनि शैलसुते || 9 ||

jaya-jaya-japya-jaye-jaya-śabda-parastuti-tatpara-viśvanute
jhaṇajhaṇa-jhiñjhimi-jhiṅkṛta-nūpura-śiñjita-mohitabhūtapate |
naṭita-naṭārdha-naṭīnaṭa-nāyaka-nāṭakanāṭita-nāṭyarate
jaya jaya he mahiśhāsura-mardini ramyakapardini śailasute || 10 ||

जय-जय-जप्य-जये-जय-शब्द-परस्तुति-तत्पर-विश्वनुते
झणझण-झिञ्झिमि-झिङ्कृत-नूपुर-शिञ्जित-मोहितभूतपते |
नटित-नटार्ध-नटीनट-नायक-नाटकनाटित-नाट्यरते
जय जय हे महिषासुर-मर्दिनि रम्यकपर्दिनि शैलसुते || 10 ||

ayi sumanaḥ sumanaḥ sumanaḥ sumanaḥ sumanohara kāntiyute
śritarajanīraja-nīraja-nīrajanī-rajanīkara-vaktravṛte |
sunayanavibhrama-rabhra-mara-bhramara-bhrama-rabhramarādhipate
jaya jaya he mahiśhāsura-mardini ramyakapardini śailasute || 11 ||

अयि सुमनः सुमनः सुमनः सुमनः सुमनोहर कान्तियुते
श्रितरजनीरज-नीरज-नीरजनी-रजनीकर-वक्त्रवृते |
सुनयनविभ्रम-रभ्र-मर-भ्रमर-भ्रम-रभ्रमराधिपते

जय जय हे महिषासुर-मर्दिनि रम्यकपर्दिनि शैलसुते || 11 ||

mahita-mahāhava-mallamatallika-
mallita-rallaka-malla-rate
virachitavallika-pallika-mallika-jhillika-
bhillika-vargavṛte |
sita-kṛtaphulla-samullasitā'ruṇa-tallaja-
pallava-sallalite
jaya jaya he mahiśhāsura-mardini
ramyakapardini śailasute || 12 ||

महित-महाहव-मल्लमतल्लिक-मल्लित-रल्लक-मल्ल-रते
विरचितवल्लिक-पल्लिक-मल्लिक-झिल्लिक-भिल्लिक-वर्गवृते |
सित-कृतफुल्ल-समुल्लसिताऽरुण-तल्लज-पल्लव-सल्ललिते
जय जय हे महिषासुर-मर्दिनि रम्यकपर्दिनि शैलसुते || 12 ||

aviraḻa-gaṇḍagaḻan-mada-medura-matta-
mataṅgajarāja-pate
tribhuvana-bhūśhaṇabhūta-
kaḻānidhirūpa-payonidhirājasute |
ayi sudatījana-lālasa-mānasa-mohana-
manmadharāja-sute
jaya jaya he mahiśhāsura-mardini
ramyakapardini śailasute || 13 ||

अविरल-गण्डगलन्-मद-मेदुर-मत्त-मतङ्गजराज-पते
त्रिभुवन-भूषणभूत-कलानिधिरूप-पयोनिधिराजसुते |
अयि सुदतीजन-लालस-मानस-मोहन-मन्मधराज-सुते

जय जय हे महिषासुर-मर्दिनि रम्यकपर्दिनि शैलसुते ॥ 13 ॥

**kamaladaḻāmala-komala-kānti-kalākalitā'mala-bhālatale
sakala-vilāsakaḻā-nilayakrama-keḻikalat-kalahaṃsakule |
alikula-saṅkula-kuvalayamaṇḍala-mauḻimilad-vakulālikule
jaya jaya he mahiśhāsura-mardini ramyakapardini śailasute || 14 ||**

कमलदलामल-कोमल-कान्ति-कलाकलिताऽमल-भालतले
सकल-विलासकला-निलयक्रम-केलिकलत्-कलहंसकुले।
अलिकुल-सङ्कुल-कुवलयमण्डल-मौलिमिलद्-वकुलालिकुले
जय जय हे महिषासुर-मर्दिनि रम्यकपर्दिनि शैलसुते ॥ 14 ॥

**kara-muraḻī-rava-vījita-kūjita-lajjita-kokila-mañjurute
milita-milinda-manohara-guñjita-rañjita-śailanikuñja-gate |
nijagaṇabhūta-mahāśabarīgaṇa-raṅgaṇa-sambhṛta-keḻitate
jaya jaya he mahiśhāsura-mardini ramyakapardini śailasute || 15 ||**

कर-मुरली-रव-वीजित-कूजित-लज्जित-कोकिल-मञ्जुरुते
मिलित-मिलिन्द-मनोहर-गुञ्जित-रञ्जित-शैलनिकुञ्ज-गते।
निजगणभूत-महाशबरीगण-रङ्गण-सम्भृत-केलितते

जय जय हे महिषासुर-मर्दिनि रम्यकपर्दिनि शैलसुते || 15 ||

kaṭitaṭa-pīta-dukūla-vichitra-mayūkha-
tiraskṛta-chandraruche
praṇatasurāsura-mauḻimaṇisphurad-
aṃśulasan-nakhasāndraruche |
jita-kanakāchalamauḻi-madorjita-
nirjarakuñjara-kumbha-kuche
jaya jaya he mahiśhāsura-mardini
ramyakapardini śailasute || 16 ||

कटितट-पीत-दुकूल-विचित्र-मयूख-तिरस्कृत-चन्द्ररुचे
प्रणतसुरासुर-मौलिमणिस्फुरद्-अंशुलसन्-नखसान्द्ररुचे |
जित-कनकाचलमौलि-मदोर्जित-निर्जरकुञ्जर-कुम्भ-कुचे
जय जय हे महिषासुर-मर्दिनि रम्यकपर्दिनि शैलसुते || 16 ||

vijita-sahasrakaraika-sahasrakaraika-
sahasrakaraikanute
kṛta-suratāraka-saṅgara-tāraka saṅgara-
tārakasūnu-sute |
suratha-samādhi-samāna-samādhi-
samādhisamādhi-sujāta-rate
jaya jaya he mahiśhāsura-mardini
ramyakapardini śailasute || 17 ||

विजित-सहस्रकरैक-सहस्रकरैक-सहस्रकरैकनुते
कृत-सुरतारक-सङ्गर-तारक सङ्गर-तारकसूनु-सुते |
सुरथ-समाधि-समान-समाधि-समाधिसमाधि-सुजात-रते

जय जय हे महिषासुर-मर्दिनि रम्यकपर्दिनि शैलसुते || 17 ||

padakamalaṃ karuṇānilaye varivasyati yoanudinaṃ na śive
ayi kamale kamalānilaye kamalānilayaḥ sa kathaṃ na bhavet |
tava padameva parampada-mityanuśīlayato mama kiṃ na śive
jaya jaya he mahiśhāsura-mardini ramyakapardini śailasute || 18 ||

पदकमलं करुणानिलये वरिवस्यति योऽनुदिनं न शिवे
अयि कमले कमलानिलये कमलानिलयः स कथं न भवेत् |
तव पदमेव परम्पद-मित्यनुशीलयतो मम किं न शिवे
जय जय हे महिषासुर-मर्दिनि रम्यकपर्दिनि शैलसुते || 18 ||

kanakalasatkala-sindhujalairanuśhiñjati te guṇaraṅgabhuvaṃ
bhajati sa kiṃ nu śachīkuchakumbhata-taṭīpari-rambha-sukhānubhavaṃ |
tava charaṇaṃ śaraṇaṃ karavāṇi natāmaravāṇi nivāśi śivaṃ
jaya jaya he mahiśhāsura-mardini ramyakapardini śailasute || 19 ||

कनकलसत्कल-सिन्धुजलैरनुषिञ्चति ते गुणरङ्गभुवं
भजति स किं नु शचीकुचकुम्भत-तटीपरि-रम्भ-सुखानुभवं |
तव चरणं शरणं करवाणि नतामरवाणि निवाशि शिवं

जय जय हे महिषासुर-मर्दिनि रम्यकपर्दिनि शैलसुते || 19 ||

tava vimaleandukalaṃ vadanendumalaṃ
sakalaṃ nanu kūlayate
kimu puruhūta-purīndumukhī-
sumukhībhirasau-vimukhī-kriyate |
mama tu mataṃ śivanāma-dhane bhavatī-
kṛpayā kimuta kriyate
jaya jaya he mahiśhāsura-mardini
ramyakapardini śailasute || 20 ||

तव विमलेऽन्दुकलं वदनेन्दुमलं सकलं ननु कूलयते
किमु पुरुहूत-पुरीन्दुमुखी-सुमुखीभिरसौ-विमुखी-क्रियते |
मम तु मतं शिवनाम-धने भवती-कृपया किमुत क्रियते
जय जय हे महिषासुर-मर्दिनि रम्यकपर्दिनि शैलसुते || 20 ||

ayi mayi dīnadayāḻutayā karuṇāparayā
bhavitavyamume
ayi jagato jananī kṛpayāsi yathāsi
tathānumitāsi rame |
yaduchitamatra bhavatyurarī kurutā-
durutāpamapā-kurute
jaya jaya he mahiśhāsura-mardini
ramyakapardini śailasute || 21 ||

अयि मयि दीनदयालुतया करुणापरया भवितव्यमुमे
अयि जगतो जननी कृपयासि यथासि तथानुमितासि रमे |
यदुचितमत्र भवत्युररी कुरुता-दुरुतापमपा-कुरुते
जय जय हे महिषासुर-मर्दिनि रम्यकपर्दिनि शैलसुते || 21 ||

The Mahishasura Mardini Stotram composed by the great sage Adi Shankaracharya around 810 AD, this stotram is based on the Devi Mahatmyam and extols the different powers (shaktis) of the Devi.

Durgā Aśhṭottara Sata Nāmāvaḻi

oṃ durgāyai namaḥ|
oṃ śivāyai namaḥ |
oṃ mahālakśhmyai namaḥ |
oṃ mahāgauryai namaḥ |
oṃ caṇḍikāyai namaḥ |
oṃ sarvaGYāyai namaḥ |
oṃ sarvālokeśyai namaḥ |
oṃ sarvakarma phalapradāyai namaḥ |
oṃ sarvatīrdha mayāyai namaḥ |
oṃ puṇyāyai namaḥ ||10||
oṃ deva yonaye namaḥ |
oṃ ayonijāyai namaḥ |
oṃ bhūmijāyai namaḥ |
oṃ nirguṇāyai namaḥ |
oṃ ādhāraśaktyai namaḥ |
oṃ anīśvaryai namaḥ |
oṃ nirguṇāyai namaḥ |
oṃ nirahaṅkārāyai namaḥ |
oṃ sarvagarvavimardinyai namaḥ |
oṃ sarvalokapriyāyai namaḥ ||20||
oṃ vāṇyai namaḥ |
oṃ sarvavidhyādi devatāyai namaḥ |

oṃ pārvatyai namaḥ |
oṃ devamātre namaḥ |
oṃ vanīśyai namaḥ |
oṃ vindhya vāsinyai namaḥ |
oṃ tejovatyai namaḥ |
oṃ mahāmātre namaḥ |
oṃ koṭisūrya samaprabhāyai namaḥ |
oṃ devatāyai namaḥ ||30||
oṃ vahnirūpāyai namaḥ |
oṃ satejase namaḥ |
oṃ varṇarūpiṇyai namaḥ |
oṃ guṇāśrayāyai namaḥ |
oṃ guṇamadhyāyai namaḥ |
oṃ guṇatrayavivarjitāyai namaḥ |
oṃ karmaGYāna pradāyai namaḥ |
oṃ kāntāyai namaḥ |
oṃ sarvasaṃhāra kāriṇyai namaḥ |
oṃ dharmaGYānāyai namaḥ ||40||
oṃ dharmaniśhṭāyai namaḥ |
oṃ sarvakarmavivarjitāyai namaḥ |
oṃ kāmākśhyai namaḥ |
oṃ kāmāsaṃhantryai namaḥ |
oṃ kāmakrodha vivarjitāyai namaḥ |
oṃ śāṅkaryai namaḥ |
oṃ śāmbhavyai namaḥ |
oṃ śāntāyai namaḥ |
oṃ candrasuryāgnilocanāyai namaḥ

oṃ sujayāyai namaḥ ||50||
oṃ jayāyai namaḥ |
oṃ bhūmiśhṭhāyai namaḥ |
oṃ jāhnavyai namaḥ |
oṃ janapūjitāyai namaḥ |
oṃ śāstrāyai namaḥ |
oṃ śāstramayāyai namaḥ |
oṃ nityāyai namaḥ |
oṃ śubhāyai namaḥ |
oṃ candrārdhamastakāyai namaḥ |
oṃ bhāratyai namaḥ ||60||
oṃ bhrāmaryai namaḥ |
oṃ kalpāyai namaḥ |
oṃ karālyai namaḥ |
oṃ kṛśhṇa piṅgalāyai namaḥ |
oṃ brāhmyai namaḥ |
oṃ nārāyaṇyai namaḥ |
oṃ raudryai namaḥ |
oṃ candrāmṛta parivṛtāyai namaḥ |
oṃ jyeśhṭhāyai namaḥ |
oṃ indirāyai namaḥ ||70||
oṃ mahāmāyāyai namaḥ |
oṃ jagatsṛśhṭyādhikāriṇyai namaḥ |
oṃ brahmāṇḍa koṭi saṃsthānāyai namaḥ |
oṃ kāminyai namaḥ |
oṃ kamalālayāyai namaḥ |
oṃ kātyāyanyai namaḥ |

oṃ kalātītāyai namaḥ |
oṃ kālasaṃhārakāriṇyai namaḥ |
oṃ yogāniśhṭhāyai namaḥ |
oṃ yogigamyāyai namaḥ ||80||
oṃ yogadhyeyāyai namaḥ |
oṃ tapasvinyai namaḥ |
oṃ GYānarūpāyai namaḥ |
oṃ nirākārāyai namaḥ |
oṃ bhaktābhīśhṭa phalapradāyai namaḥ |
oṃ bhūtātmikāyai namaḥ |
oṃ bhūtamātre namaḥ |
oṃ bhūteśyai namaḥ |
oṃ bhūtadhāriṇyai namaḥ |
oṃ svadhānārī madhyagatāyai namaḥ
||90||
oṃ śhaḍādhārādhi vardhinyai namaḥ |
oṃ mohitāyai namaḥ |
oṃ aṃśubhavāyai namaḥ |
oṃ śubhrāyai namaḥ |
oṃ sūkśhmāyai namaḥ |
oṃ mātrāyai namaḥ |
oṃ nirālasāyai namaḥ |
oṃ nimagnāyai namaḥ |
oṃ nīlasaṅkāśāyai namaḥ |
oṃ nityānandinyai namaḥ ||100||
oṃ harāyai namaḥ |
oṃ parāyai namaḥ |

oṃ sarvaGYānapradāyai namaḥ |
oṃ anantāyai namaḥ |
oṃ satyāyai namaḥ |
oṃ durlabha rūpiṇyai namaḥ |
oṃ sarasvatyai namaḥ |
oṃ sarvagatāyai namaḥ |
oṃ sarvābhīśhṭapradāyinyai namaḥ || 108 ||

Ashtottara Shatanamavali means collective hundred and eight names of God or Goddess. 108 has been considered a sacred number in Hinduism.We find many Ashtottara Shatanamavalis in Purana as well as in epics like Mahabharata. These names are composed by Rishis, devotees, divine beings etc.

One of the benefits of chanting this Durgā Aśhṭottara Sata Nāmāvaḻi dissolves all the difficulties you are facing in your personal and professional life.

Prayer

Om Sarve Bhavantu Sukhinah
Sarve Santu Nir-Aamayaah |
Sarve Bhadraanni Pashyantu
Maa Kashcid-Duhkha-Bhaag-Bhavet |
Om Shaantih Shaantih Shaantih ||

ॐ सर्वे भवन्तु सुखिनः
सर्वे सन्तु निरामयाः ।
सर्वे भद्राणि पश्यन्तु
मा कश्चिद्दुःखभाग्भवेत् ।
ॐ शान्तिः शान्तिः शान्तिः ॥

Om, May All be prosperous and happy. May All be Free

from Illness.May All See what is Auspicious and spiritu-ally uplifting. May Nobody suffer.Om Peace, Peace, Peace.

*****

BOOK: 2 MAA LAKSHMI PUJA

LIST OF POWERFUL SACRED MANTRAS FOR LAKSHMI PUJA (INDEX)

- ✓ ***Lakshmi Beej(ah) Mantra***
- ✓ ***Lakshmi Gayatri Mantra***
- ✓ ***Five Powerful mantras of Maa Lakshmi that brings progress in your life***
    1. *Mantra For for Business Success*
    2. *Mantra for Career/Job Success*
    3. *Mantra for Mantra for wealth and abundance.*
    4. *Mantra for good fortune*
    5. *Mantra for happiness*
- ✓ ***Sri Mahalakshmi Ashtakam***
- ✓ ***Stotram :*** *Kanakadhāra Stotram*
- ✓ ***Namavali*** *: Mahālakshmi Aśhṭottara Sata Nāmāvaḻi*
- ✓ ***Prayer Mantra (Prarthna)***

***

GODDESS LAKSHMI

The word 'Lakshmi' first mentioned in the Śrī Sūkta of the Rigveda. The name "Lakshmi" is derived from the Sanskrit word "Laksya"signifies 'aspire' (aim or goal). She is the goddess of wealth and prosperity. According to the Hindu Puranas, Maa Lakshmi (Shri) was the daughter of the sage Bhrigu and his wife Khyati. She is the consort of Vishnu, called MahaLakshmi. Lakshmi is known to be very closely associated with the lotus, and her many epithets are connected to the flower.Her four hands signify her power to grant the four object of human pursuit, Righteousness(Dharma), Wealth (Artha) , Pleasures of the flesh(Kama), and a Beatitude-supreme happiness (Moksha).Representations of Lakshmi are also found in Jainsm and in Buddhism. Whenever you wish to start something new, praying to Goddess Lakhmi will give you all the success.

Puja and Festival Celebration dedicated to Maa Lakshmi (Mahalakshmi)

- Varalakshmi Vrata - Varamahalakshmi Puja(Last Friday Shravana Poornima)
- Gaja Lakshmi Puja (First nine days of the Ashwin Shukla Paksha)
- Kojagari Lakshmi Puja (Ashwin Poornima)
- Deepavali - Lakshmi Puja (Ashwin Krishna Paksha Amavasya)

- Navrathiri (Four, five and sixth days of Navaratri)
- New moonday, Full Moon Day, Thursday, Friday

(Note: Please check and verify exact dates of festival celebrations in Hindu calendars or Panchang)

***

MAA LAKSHMI PUJA MANTRAS

"Let Goddess Maha Lakshmi bless you with all eight forces on this Puja : Shri (Wealth), Bhu (Earth), Saraswati (learning), Priti (love), Kirti (Fame), Shanti (Peace), Tushti (Pleasure) and Pushti (Strength"

Invocation to Lord Ganesh

Vakra-Tunndda Maha-Kaaya Suurya-Kotti Samaprabha |
Nirvighnam Kuru Me Deva Sarva-Kaaryessu Sarvadaa ||

वक्रतुण्ड महाकाय सूर्यकोटि समप्रभ ।
निर्विघ्नं कुरु मे देव सर्वकार्येषु सर्वदा ॥

Salutations to Sri Ganesha : O Lord, Who has a Curved Trunk, Who has a Large Body, Whose aura is like light of crores of sun, Please make my entire work obstacle free, forever.

Chanting of this mantra helps to achieve wealth, wisdom, good luck, prosperity and success in all the endeavors.

Shanthi Mantra

Om Saha Naav (au)-Avatu |
Saha Nau Bhunaktu |
Saha Viiryam Karavaavahai |

Tejasvi Naav[au]Adhii tam-Astu Maa Vidvissaavahai |
Om Shaantih: Shaantih: Shaantih: ||

ॐ सह नाववतु ।
सह नौ भुनक्तु ।
सह वीर्यं करवावहै ।
तेजस्वि नावधीतमस्तु मा विद्विषावहै ।
ॐ शान्तिः शान्तिः शान्तिः ॥

Om, May He protect us both together; may He nourish us both togethe.Together may we perform . May what has been Studied by us be vigorous and effective; .Om! Let there be peace in me! May peace be unto us, and may peace be unto all living beings.

This Shanti mantra, prayer for peace found in the krishna Yajurveda Taittiriya Upanishad (2.2.2).This mantra purifies the body and relieves it from the sufferings, diseases and discomforts.

Asana Puja

Om Prthvi Tvayaa Dhrtaa Lokaa
Devi Tvam Vissnnunaa Dhrtaa |
Tvam Ca Dhaaraya Maam Devi
Pavitram Kuru Ca-[A]asanam ||

ॐ पृथ्वि त्वया धृता लोका
देवि त्वं विष्णुना धृता ।
त्वं च धारय मां देवि
पवित्रं कुरु चासनम् ॥

Om, O Prithivi Devi /Bhoomi Devi, You are borne the entire world Please hold me O Devi, and make this seat of the worshipper Pure.

Deepa Puja

Shubham Karoti Kalyaannam-Aarogyam Dhana-Sampadaa |
Shatru-Buddhi-Vinaashaaya Diipa-Jyotir-Namostute ||

शुभं करोति कल्याणमारोग्यं धनसंपदा ।
शत्रुबुद्धिविनाशाय दीपज्योतिर्नमोऽस्तुते ॥

Salutations to the Light of the Lamp, Which Brings Auspiciousness, Health and Prosperity; Which Destroys Inimical Feelings

Gayatri Mantra for Pranayama

Om Bhuuh : Om Bhuvah: Om Svah:
Om Mahah :Om Janah : Om Tapah: Om Satyam
Om Tat-Savitur Varennyam Bhargo Devasya Dhiimahi
Dhiyo Yo Nah Pracodayaat |
Om Aapo Jyotii Rasoa Amrtam
Brahma Bhuur Bhuvah: SvarOm ||

(Touch the ears three times and saying Om, Om , Om)

ॐ भूः ॐ भुवः ॐ स्वः
ॐ महः ॐ जनः ॐ तपः ॐ सत्यम्
ॐ तत्सवितुर्वरेण्यं भर्गो देवस्य धीमहि

धियो यो नः प्रचोदयात् ।
ॐ आपो ज्योती रसोऽमृतं ब्रह्म भूर्भुवः स्वरोम् ॥

Yajur Veda: Taittiriya Aranyaka

Om,I meditate on the Consciousness of the Physical Plane, Om, I meditate on the intercede Space, Om, I meditate on the Heaven, Consciousness of the beginning of the Divine Mind.(the meditation goes to subtler levels)

This strengthens our mind with concentration and gives immense peace to us.

SANKALPA MANTRA

For Saivas :

Mamo partha samastha duritha kshaya dwara ,

Sri Parameshwara preethyartham

Sri Mahalakshmi prasada sidhyartham

Asmaham Sakudumbanam

shemasya, dhairyasya, dhairya, vijaya, ayur, arogya, ishwarya, abhiv-rithyartham, Kalyana Prapyartham, Sakala vasikaranartham

Mahaganaptim pujam karishye

For Vaishnavas:

Mamo partha samastha duritha kshaya dwara ,

Sri Narayana Preethyartham

Sri Mahalakshmi prasada sidhyartham

Asmaham Sakudumbanam

shemasya, dhairyasya, dhairya, vijaya, ayur, arogya, ishwarya, abhiv-rithyartham, Kalyana Prapyartham, Sakala vasikaranartham

Mahaganaptim pujam karishye

Om For removing all problems and pains in life.For making Lord happy. For blessings of Goddess Parvathi. For getting my above wishes fulfilled.

The procedure of making a decision to perform the pooja for the welfare of all concerned.

Kalash(a) Puja

Kalashasya mukhe Vishnu: kanTe rudrassamaasrita:|
Mule tatra sthitho brahma madhye matrugana: smruta: ||
kukshou thu saagara: sarve sapthadveepa vasundhara: |
Rigvedoatha yajurveda: saama vedo atharvavana: ||
angaischa sahita ssarve kalashaambu samaasrita: |

कलशस्य मुखे विष्णु: कण्ठे रुद्र: समाश्रित:|

मूले तस्य स्थितो ब्रह्मा मध्ये मातृगणाः स्थिता ||
कुक्षौ तु सागरः सर्वे सप्तद्वीपा वसुन्धरा |
ग्वेंदो यजुर्वेदः सामवेदो अथर्वणः ||
अङ्गैश्च सहितं सर्वे कलशाम्बु समाश्रिताः |

Kalash(a) is traditionally a copper pot. Fill it up with water and put two or three leaves of tulsi leaves or flower petals as well . Take few more couple of flower petals (or Tulsi leaves) dip it in the pot water and sprinkle it around the area you are seated . Then sprinkle the few drops of water if,other people seated around you .

Invite all the holy rivers like Ganga,yamuna, saraswati,narmada, godavari, sindhu,kaveri into this water pot . Invite all the gods ie Brahma, Vishnu, Shiva, Ganesh. (May come to me to bestow Peace and remove the Evil Influences)

Ghanta Puja

Aagama Artham Tu Devaanaam Gamana Artham Tu Rakssasaam |
Ghannttaa Ravam Karomya(ia)adau Devataa Ahvaana Laan chanam ||

आगमार्थं तु देवानां गमनार्थं तु रक्षसाम् ।
घण्टारवं करोम्यादौ देवताह्वान लाञ्छनम् ॥

For the purpose of inviting the Divine Forces and removing Evil Forces, I make the (Ghanta) Bell Sound.

Mahalakshmi Mantra

**Om Sarvabaadhaa Vinirmukto,
Dhan Dhaanyah: Sutaanvitah: |
Manushyo Matprasaaden Bhavishyati
Na Sanshayah : Om ||**

ॐ सर्वाबाधा विनिर्मुक्तो, धन धान्यः सुतान्वितः।
मनुष्यो मत्प्रसादेन भविष्यति न संशयः ॐ ।।

O Goddess Mahalakshmi, eradicate all evil forces and bestow upon all a prosperous and Wealth

(Note: You can chant this mantra 3 or 9 or 18 times to get more benefit)

Lakshmi Beej(ah) Mantra

|| Om Shring Shriye(a) Namah ||

।। ॐ श्रीं श्रियें नमः ।।

***This** Beej (ah) Mantra is considered as origin of all powers of Goddess Lakshmi. The Mantra of Goddess Lakshmi is only Shring(श्रीं), which is combined with other words to form various Mantras.*

(Note: You can chant this mantra 3 or 9 or 18 times to get more benefit)

Lakshmi Gayatri Mantra

**Om Shree Mahalakshmyai Cha Vidmahe
Vishnu Patnyai Cha Dheemahi
Tanno Lakshmi Prachodayat Om ||**

ॐ श्री महालक्ष्म्यै च विद्महे विष्णु पत्नै च धीमहि

तन्नो लक्ष्मी प्रचोदयात् ॐ॥

Om, Let me meditate on the greatest goddess, Who is the wife of Lord Vishnu, provide me higher intellect, And let Goddess Lakshmi make brighter my mind.

*(Note: You can chant this mantra 3 or 9 or 18 times to get **prosperity and success.**)*

Five Powerful mantras of Maa Lakshmi that brings progress in your life

Mantra for Business Success

Om ain shreen mahaalakshmyai kamal dhaarinyai garood vaahinyai shreen ain namah:

ॐ ऐं श्रीं महालक्ष्म्यै कमल धारिण्यै गरूड़ वाहिन्यै श्रीं ऐं नमः

Mantra for Career/Job Success

Om Hring Shring Kreeng Shring Kreeng Kling Shring Mahaalakshmi Mam Grihe Dhanam Pooray Pooray Chintaayai Dooray Dooray Swaha |

ॐ ह्री श्रीं क्रीं श्रीं क्रीं क्लीं श्रीं महालक्ष्मी मम गृहे धनं
पूरय पूरय चिंतायै दूरय दूरय स्वाहा ।

Mantra for Mantra for wealth and abundance.

Om Shreem Maha Lakshmiyei Namah:

ॐ श्रीं महालक्ष्म्यै नमः

Mantra for good fortune

om shreen hreen kleen:

ॐ श्रीं ह्रीं क्लीं:

Mantra for happiness

Om Shreen Shree-aee Namaha

ॐ श्रीं श्रीय नम:

(Note: You can chant these mantras 3 or 9 or 18 times to get more benefit)

Sri Mahalakshmi Ashtakam

Namastestu Mahaa-Maaye Shrii-Piitthe Sura-Puujite |
Shangkha-Cakra-Gadaa-Haste Mahaalakssmi Namostute ||1||

नमस्तेऽस्तु महामाये श्रीपीठे सुरपूजिते ।
शङ्खचक्रगदाहस्ते महालक्ष्मि नमोऽस्तुते ॥१॥

Namaste Garudda-Aaruuddhe Kola-Aasura-Bhayamkari |
Sarva-Paapa-Hare Devi Mahaalakssmi Namostute ||2||

नमस्ते गरुडारूढे कोलासुरभयंकरि ।
सर्वपापहरे देवि महालक्ष्मि नमोऽस्तुते ॥२॥

Sarvajnye Sarva-Varade Sarva-Dusstta-Bhayamkari |

Sarva-Duhkha-Hare Devi Mahaalakssmi Namostute ||3||

सर्वज्ञे सर्ववरदे सर्वदुष्टभयंकरि ।

सर्वदुःखहरे देवि महालक्ष्मि नमोऽस्तुते ॥३॥

Siddhi-Buddhi-Prade Devi Bhukti-Mukti-Pradaayini |
Mantra-Muurte Sadaa Devi Mahaalakssmi Namostute ||4||

सिद्धिबुद्धिप्रदे देवि भुक्तिमुक्तिप्रदायिनि ।
मन्त्रमूर्ते सदा देवि महालक्ष्मि नमोऽस्तुते ॥४॥

Aad-Anta-Rahite Devi Aadya-Shakti-Maheshvari |
Yogaje Yoga-Sambhuute Mahaalakssmi Namostute ||5||

आद्यन्तरहिते देवि आद्यशक्तिमहेश्वरि ।
योगजे योगसम्भूते महालक्ष्मि नमोऽस्तुते ॥५॥

Sthuula-Suukssma-Mahaaroudre Mahaa-Shakti-Mahodare |
Mahaa-Paapa-Hare Devi Mahaalakssmi Namostute ||6||

स्थूलसूक्ष्ममहारौद्रे महाशक्तिमहोदरे ।
महापापहरे देवि महालक्ष्मि नमोऽस्तुते ॥६॥

Padma-Aasana-Sthite Devi Para-Brahma-Svaruupinni |
Parameshi Jagan-Maatar-Mahaalakssmi Namostute ||7||

पद्मासनस्थिते देवि परब्रह्मस्वरूपिणि ।

परमेशि जगन्मातर्महालक्ष्मि नमोऽस्तुते ॥७॥

**Shveta-Ambara-Dhare Devi Naana-Alangkaara-Bhuussite |
Jagatsthite Jagan-Maatar-Mahaalakssmi Namostute ||8||**

श्वेताम्बरधरे देवि नानालङ्कारभूषिते ।
जगत्स्थिते जगन्मातर्महालक्ष्मि नमोऽस्तुते ॥८॥

**Mahaalakssmyassttakam Stotram Yah: Patthedbhaktimaannarah: |
Sarvasiddhimavaapnoti Raajyam Praapnoti Sarvadaa ||9||**

महालक्ष्म्यष्टकं स्तोत्रं यः पठेद्भक्तिमान्नरः ।
सर्वसिद्धिमवाप्नोति राज्यं प्राप्नोति सर्वदा ॥९॥

**Ekakaale Patthennityam Mahaapaapavinaashanam |
Dvikaalam Yah Patthennityam Dhanadhaanyasamanvitah: ||10||**

एककाले पठेन्नित्यं महापापविनाशनम् ।
द्विकालं यः पठेन्नित्यं धनधान्यसमन्वितः ॥१०॥

**Trikaalam Yah: Patthennityam Mahaashatruvinaashanam |
Mahaalakssmirbhavennityam Prasannaa Varadaa Shubhaa ||11||**

त्रिकालं यः पठेन्नित्यं महाशत्रुविनाशनम् ।
महालक्ष्मिर्भवेन्नित्यं प्रसन्ना वरदा शुभा ॥११॥

Shri Mahalakshmi Ashtakam is taken from 'Padma Purana 'and this prayer was chanted by Lord Indra. This prayer is very ancient and has been chanted by generations for solving all their problems.

Kanakadhāra Stotram

Angam hare: pulaka bhooshanamasray-anthi,
Bhringanga neva mukulabharanam thamalam |
Angikrithakhila vibhuthirapanga leela,
Mangalyadasthu mama mangala devathaya: || 1||

अङ्गं हरेः पुलकभूषणमाश्रयन्ती
भृङ्गाङ्गनेव मुकुलाभरणं तमालम् ।
अंगीकृताखिलविभूतिरपांगलीला
मांगल्यदास्तु मम मंगलदेवतायाः ॥ १ ॥

Mugdha muhurvidhadhadathi vadhane Murare:
Premathrapapranihithani gathagathani |
Mala dhrishotmadhukareeva maheth pale ya,
Sa ne sriyam dhisathu sagarasambhavaya: ||2||

मुग्धा मुहुर्विदधती वदने मुरारेः
प्रेमत्रपाप्रणिहितानि गतागतानि ।

माला दृशोर्मधुकरीव महोत्पले या
सा मे श्रियं दिशतु सागरसंभवायाः ॥ २ ॥

Ameelithaksha madhigamya mudha Mukundam
Anandakandamanimeshamananga thanthram,
Akekara stiththa kaninika pashma nethram,
Bhoothyai bhavenmama bhjan-gasayananganaya : || 3||

आमीलिताक्षमधिगम्य मुदा मुकुन्दं
आनन्दकन्दमनिमेषमनंगतन्त्रम् ।
आकेकरस्थितकनीनिकपक्ष्मनेत्रं
भूत्यै भवेन्मम भुजंगशयांगनायाः ॥ ३ ॥

Bahwanthare madhujitha: srithakausthube ya,
Haravaleeva nari neela mayi vibhathi,
Kamapradha bhagavatho api kadaksha mala,
Kalyanamavahathu me kamalalayaya: || 4 ||

बाह्वन्तरे मधुजितः श्रितकौस्तुभे या
हारावलीव हरिनीलमयी विभाति ।

कामप्रदा भगवतोऽपि कटाक्षमाला
कल्याणमावहतु मे कमलालयायाः ॥ ४ ॥

**Kalambudhaalithorasi kaida bhare:
Dharaadhare sphurathi yaa thadinganeva
|
Mathu samastha jagatham mahaneeya murthy :
Badrani me dhisathu bhargava nandanaya : || 5 ||**

कालाम्बुदालिललितोरसि कैटभारेः
धाराधरे स्फुरति या तटिदङ्गनेव ।
मातुस्समस्तजगतां महनीयमूर्तिः
भद्राणि मे दिशतु भार्गवनन्दनायाः ॥ ५ ॥

**Praptham padam pradhamatha khalu yat prabhavath,
Mangalyabhaji madhu madhini manamathena |
Mayyapadetha mathara meekshanardham,
Manthalasam cha makaralaya kanyakaya: || 6 ||**

प्राप्तं पदं प्रथमतः खलु यत्प्रभावात्
माङ्गल्यभाजि मधुमाथिनि मन्मथेन ।
मयापतेत्तदिह मन्थरमीक्षणार्धं
मन्दालसं च मकरालयकन्यकायाः ॥ ६ ॥

Viswamarendra padhavee bramadhana dhaksham,
Ananda hethu radhikam madhu vishwoapi |
Eshanna sheedhathu mayi kshanameek-shanartham,
Indhivarodhara sahodhar-amidhiraya : || 7 ||

विश्वामरेन्द्रपदविभ्रमदानदक्षं
आनन्दहेतुरधिकं मुरविद्विषोऽपि ।
ईषन्निषीदतु मयि क्षणमीक्षणार्धं
इन्दीवरोदरसहोदरमिन्दिरायाः ॥ ७ ॥

Ishta visishtamathayopi yaya dhayardhra,
Dhrishtya thravishta papadam sulabham labhanthe |
Hrishtim prahrushta kamlodhara deepthirishtam,
Pushtim krishishta mama pushkravishtaraya: || 8 ||

इष्टा विशिष्टमतयोऽपि यया दयार्द्र-
दृष्ट्या त्रिविष्टपपदं सुलभं लभन्ते ।
दृष्टिः प्रहृष्टकमलोदरदीप्तिरिष्टां
पुष्टिं कृषीष्ट मम पुष्करविष्टरायाः ॥ ८ ॥

Dhadyaddhayanupavanopi dravinambhudaraam,
Asminna kinchina vihanga sisou vishanne |
Dhushkaramagarmmapaneeya chiraya dhooram,
Narayana pranayinee nayanambhuvaha: || 9 ||

दद्याद्दयानुपवनो द्रविणाम्बुधारां
अस्मिन्नकिञ्चनविहंगशिशौ विषण्णे ।
दुष्कर्मघर्ममपनीय चिराय दूरं
नारायणप्रणयिनीनयनाम्बुवाहः ॥ ९ ॥

Gheerdhevathethi garuda dwaja sundarithi,
Sakambhareethi sasi shekara vallebhethi |
Srishti sthithi pralaya kelishu samsthitha ya,
Thasyai namas thribhvanai ka guros tharunyai: || 10 ||

गीर्देवतेति गरुडध्वजसुन्दरीति
शाकंभरीति शशिशेखरवल्लभेति ।
सृष्टिस्थितिप्रलयकेलिषु संस्थितायै
तस्यै नमस्त्रिभुवनैकगुरोस्तरुण्यै ॥ १० ॥

Sruthyai namosthu shubha karma phala prasoothyai,
Rathyai namosthu ramaneeya gunarnavayai |
Shakthyai namosthu satha pathra nikethanayai,
Pushtayi namosthu purushotthama vallabhayai: || 11 ||

श्रुत्यै नमोऽस्तु शुभकर्मफलप्रसूत्यै
रत्यै नमोऽस्तु रमणीयगुणार्णवायै ।
शक्त्यै नमोऽस्तु शतपत्रनिकेतनायै
पुष्ट्यै नमोऽस्तु पुरुषोत्तमवल्लभायै ॥ ११ ॥

Namosthu naleekha nibhananai,
Namosthu dhugdhogdhadhi janma bhoomayai |
Namosthu somamrutha sodharayai,
Namosthu narayana vallabhayai: || 12 ||

नमोऽस्तु नालीकनिभाननायै
नमोऽस्तु दुग्धोदधिजन्मभूम्यै ।
नमोऽस्तु सोमामृतसोदरायै
नमोऽस्तु नारायणवल्लभायै ॥ १२ ॥

Namosthu hemambhuja peetikayai,
Namosthu bhoo mandala nayikayai |

Namosthu devathi dhaya prayai,
Namosthu Sarngayudha
vallabhayai: || 13 ||

नमोऽस्तु हेमाम्बुजपीठिकायै
नमोऽस्तु भूमण्डलनायिकायै ।
नमोऽस्तु देवादिदयापरायै
नमोऽस्तु शाङ्गार्युधवल्लभायै ॥ १३ ॥

Namosthu devyai bhrugu nandanayai,
Namosthu vishnorurasi sthithayai |
Namosthu lakshmyai kamalalayai,
Namosthu dhamodhra vallabhayai: || 14 ||

नमोऽस्तु देव्यै भृगुनन्दनायै
नमोऽस्तु विष्णोरुरसि स्थितायै ।
नमोऽस्तु लक्ष्म्यै कमलालयायै
नमोऽस्तु दामोदरवल्लभायै ॥ १४ ॥

Namosthu Kanthyai kamalekshanayai,
Namosthu bhoothyai bhuvanaprasoothyai
|
Namosthu devadhibhir archithayai,
Namosthu nandhathmaja
vallabhayai: || 15 ||

नमोऽस्तु कान्त्यै कमलेक्षणायै

नमोऽस्तु भूत्यै भुवनप्रसूत्यै ।
नमोऽस्तु देवादिभिरर्चितायै
नमोऽस्तु नन्दात्मजवल्लभायै ॥ १५ ॥

Sampath karaani sakalendriya nandanani,
Samrajya dhana vibhavani saroruhakshi |
Twad vandanani dhuritha harano-dhythani,
Mamev matharanisam kalayanthu manye: || 16 ||

सम्पत्कराणि सकलेन्द्रियनन्दनानि
साम्राज्यदानविभवानि सरोरुहाक्षि ।
त्वद्वन्दनानि दुरिताहरणोद्यतानि
मामेव मातरनिशं कलयन्तु मान्ये ॥ १६ ॥

Yath Kadaksha samupasana vidhi :
Sevakasya sakalartha sapadha: |
Santhanodhi vachananga manasai :
Twaam murari hridayeswareem bhaje: || 17 ||

यत्कटाक्षसमुपासनाविधिः
सेवकस्यसकलार्थसंपदः ।
सन्तनोतिवचनाङ्गमानसैः
त्वां मुरारि हृदयेश्वरीं भजे ॥ १७ ॥

Sarasija nilaye saroja hasthe,
Dhavalathamamsuka gandha maya shobhe |
Bhagavathi hari vallabhe manogne,
Tribhuvana bhoothikari praseeda mahye : || 18 ||

सरसिजनिलये सरोजहस्ते
धवलतरांशुकगन्धमाल्यशोभे ।
भगवति हरिवल्लभे मनोज्ञे
त्रिभुवनभूतिकरि प्रसीद मह्यम् ॥ १८ ॥

Dhiggasthibhi kanaka kumbha mukha vasrushta,
Sarvahini vimala charu jalaapluthangim |
Prathar namami jagathaam janani masesha-
Lokadhinatha grahini mamrithabhi puthreem: || 19 ||

दिग्घस्तिभिः कनककुम्भमुखावसृष्ट-
स्वर्वाहिनीविमलचारुजलाप्लुताङ्गीम् ।
प्रातर्नमामि जगतां जननीमशेष-
लोकाधिनाथगृहिणीममृताब्धिपुत्रीम् ॥ १९ ॥

Kamale Kamalaksha vallabhe twam,
Karuna poora tharingithaira pangai :|

Avalokaya mamakinchananam,
Prathamam pathamakrithrimam
dhyaya : || 20 ||

कमले कमलाक्षवल्लभे त्वं
करुणापूरतरङ्गितैरपाङ्गैः ।
अवलोकय मामकिञ्चनानां
प्रथमं पात्रमकृत्रिमं दयायाः ॥ २० ॥

Sthuvanthi ye sthuthibhirameeranwa-
ham,
Thrayeemayim thribhuvanamatharam
ramam |
Gunadhika guruthara bhagya bhagina :
Bhavanthi the bhuvi budha
bhavithasayo: || 21 ||

स्तुवन्ति ये स्तुतिभिरमीभिरन्वहं
त्रयीमयीं त्रिभुवनमातरं रमाम् ।
गुणाधिका गुरुतरभाग्यभागिनः
भवन्ति ते भुवि बुधभाविताशयाः ॥ २१ ॥

Kanakadhara Stotram, which was composed by one of India's foremost spiritual saints, Sri Adi Shankaracharya, around 810 AD. He dedicated the Stotram to Goddess Lakshmi, set in 21 hymns. Kanak means gold, and Dhara means flow. The Kanakadhara Stotram describes the beauty, grace, wisdom, and power of the Goddess of wealth and prosperity.Chant this Kanakadhara Stotram on every Fridays, and mornings and evenings on Full Moon days. This powerful Hymns helps eliminate poverty and bring happiness also push away negative energy.

Mahalakshmi Aśhṭotara Sata Nāmāvaḻi

oṃ prakṛtyai namaḥ |

oṃ vikṛtyai namaḥ |

oṃ vidyāyai namaḥ |

oṃ sarvabhūtahitapradāyai namaḥ |

oṃ śraddhāyai namaḥ |

oṃ vibhūtyai namaḥ |

oṃ surabhyai namaḥ |

oṃ paramātmikāyai namaḥ |

oṃ vāce namaḥ |

oṃ padmālayāyai namaḥ |10|

oṃ padmāyai namaḥ |

oṃ śucyai namaḥ |

oṃ svāhāyai namaḥ |

oṃ svadhāyai namaḥ |

oṃ sudhāyai namaḥ |

oṃ dhanyāyai namaḥ |

oṃ hiraṇmayyai namaḥ |

oṃ lakṣmyai namaḥ |

oṃ nityapuṣṭāyai namaḥ |
oṃ vibhāvaryai namaḥ |20|
oṃ adityai namaḥ |
oṃ dityai namaḥ |
oṃ dīptāyai namaḥ |
oṃ vasudhāyai namaḥ |
oṃ vasudhāriṇyai namaḥ |
oṃ kamalāyai namaḥ |
oṃ kāntāyai namaḥ |
oṃ kāmākṣyai namaḥ |
oṃ krodhasambhavāyai namaḥ |
oṃ anugrahaparāyai namaḥ |30|
oṃ ṛddhaye namaḥ |
oṃ anaghāyai namaḥ |
oṃ harivallabhāyai namaḥ |
oṃ aśokāyai namaḥ |
oṃ amṛtāyai namaḥ |
oṃ dīptāyai namaḥ |
oṃ lokaśoka vināśinyai namaḥ |
oṃ dharmanilayāyai namaḥ |
oṃ karuṇāyai namaḥ |
oṃ lokamātre namaḥ |40|

oṃ padmapriyāyai namaḥ |
oṃ padmahastāyai namaḥ |
oṃ padmākṣyai namaḥ |
oṃ padmasundaryai namaḥ |
oṃ padmodbhavāyai namaḥ |
oṃ padmamukhyai namaḥ |
oṃ padmanābhapriyāyai namaḥ |
oṃ ramāyai namaḥ |
oṃ padmamālādharāyai namaḥ |
oṃ devyai namaḥ|50|
oṃ padminyai namaḥ |
oṃ padmaganthinyai namaḥ |
oṃ puṇyagandhāyai namaḥ |
oṃ suprasannāyai namaḥ |
oṃ prasādābhimukhyai namaḥ |
oṃ prabhāyai namaḥ |
oṃ candravadanāyai namaḥ |
oṃ candrāyai namaḥ |
oṃ candrasahodaryai namaḥ |
oṃ caturbhujāyai namaḥ |60|
oṃ candrarūpāyai namaḥ |
oṃ indirāyai namaḥ |

oṃ induśītulāyai namaḥ |
oṃ āhlodajananyai namaḥ |
oṃ puṣṭyai namaḥ |
oṃ śivāyai namaḥ |
oṃ śivakaryai namaḥ |
oṃ satyai namaḥ |
oṃ vimalāyai namaḥ |
oṃ viśvajananyai namaḥ |70|
oṃ tuṣṭyai namaḥ |
oṃ dāridrya nāśinyai namaḥ |
oṃ prītipuṣkariṇyai namaḥ |
oṃ śāntāyai namaḥ |
oṃ śuklamālyāmbarāyai namaḥ |
oṃ śriyai namaḥ |
oṃ bhāskaryai namaḥ |
oṃ bilvanilayāyai namaḥ |
oṃ varārohāyai namaḥ |
oṃ yaśasvinyai namaḥ |80|
oṃ vasundharāyai namaḥ |
oṃ udārāṅgāyai namaḥ |
oṃ hariṇyai namaḥ |
oṃ hemamālinyai namaḥ |

oṃ dhanadhānya karyai namaḥ |

oṃ siddhaye namaḥ |

oṃ straiṇa saumyāyai namaḥ |

oṃ śubhapradāyai namaḥ |

oṃ nṛpaveśma gatānandāyai namaḥ |

oṃ varalakṣmyai namaḥ |90|

oṃ vasupradāyai namaḥ |

oṃ śubhāyai namaḥ |

oṃ hiraṇyaprākārāyai namaḥ |

oṃ samudra tanayāyai namaḥ |

oṃ jayāyai namaḥ |

oṃ maṅgaḷāyai namaḥ |

oṃ devyai namaḥ |

oṃ viṣṇu vakṣaḥsthala sthitāyai namaḥ |

oṃ viṣṇupatnyai namaḥ |

oṃ prasannākṣyai namaḥ |100|

oṃ nārāyaṇa samāśritāyai namaḥ |

oṃ dāridrya dhvaṃsinyai namaḥ |

oṃ sarvopadrava vāriṇyai namaḥ |

oṃ navadurgāyai namaḥ |

oṃ mahākāḷyai namaḥ |

oṃ brahma viṣṇu śivātmikāyai namaḥ |

oṃ trikāla ṅñāna sampannāyai namaḥ |

oṃ bhuvaneśvaryai namaḥ |108|

Ashtottara Shatanamavali means collective hundred and eight names of God or Goddess. 108 has been considered a sacred number in Hinduism.We find many Ashtottara Shatanamavalis in Puranas as well as in epics like Mahabharata. These names are composed by Rishis, devotees, divine beings etc.

This Mahalakshmi Asthotara Sata Namavali comprises of the 108 names of Goddess Lakshmi and it is advised for everyone looking for positivity and to gain high and pure happiness. Chanting this mantra will bring youth, beauty, happiness and money to one, which will make a great difference in life.

Prayer

Om Sarve Bhavantu Sukhinah
Sarve Santu Nir-Aamayaah |
Sarve Bhadraanni Pashyantu
Maa Kashcid-Duhkha-Bhaag-Bhavet |
Om Shaantih Shaantih Shaantih ||

ॐ सर्वे भवन्तु सुखिनः
सर्वे सन्तु निरामयाः ।
सर्वे भद्राणि पश्यन्तु
मा कश्चिद्दुःखभाग्भवेत् ।
ॐ शान्तिः शान्तिः शान्तिः ॥

Om, May All be prosperous and happy. May All be Free from Illness.May All See what is Auspicious and spiritu-ally uplifting. May Nobody suffer.Om Peace, Peace, Peace.

*****

BOOK:3 MAA SARASVATĪ PUJA

LIST OF POWERFUL SACRED MANTRAS FOR SARASVATĪ PUJA (INDEX)

Common Mantras for All pujas

- ✓ ***Invocation to Lord Ganesh***
- ✓ ***Shanthi Mantra** : Mantra for Peace*
- ✓ ***Asana Puja** : Worship the place for sitting*
- ✓ ***Deepa Puja** :Worship of Lamp)*
- ✓ ***Gayatri Mantra for Pranayama** : Purification of the Life Force*
- ✓ ***Sankalpa** :Oath (Promise),Resolving to perform the Puja*
- ✓ ***Kalash(a) Pooja** :Invocation of the Holy Waters in the Kalash(a)/pot*
- ✓ ***Ghanta Puja** : Worship of the Bell*

Mantras for Maa Sarasvatī Puja

- ✓ ***Sarasvatī Dhyana Mantra***
- ✓ ***Sarasvatī Beej(ah) Mantra***

- ✓ ***Sarasvatī Vidhya Mantra***
- ✓ ***Sarasvatī Gayathri Mantra***
- ✓ ***Four Powerful mantras of Maa Sarasvatī that solve all your Prayer***
    1. *Mantra For Intelligence*
    2. *Mantra for wealth and Knowledge to Gain Wisdom*
    3. *Rig Veda Mantra for illumination*
    4. *Mantra for gaining knowledge*
- ✓ ***Sarasvatī Vandana***
- ✓ ***Sharada Bhujanga Prayathashtakam***
- ✓ ***Namavali :*** *Sarasvatīi Aśhṭottara Sata Nāmāvaḻi*
- ✓ ***Prayer Mantra (Prarthna)***

***

GODDESS SARASVATĪ

Saraswati, is from Sanskrit fusion word of 'Sara' which means essence, and 'Swa ' means one self. The meaning of Saraswati is "one who leads to essence of self-knowledge. 'Surasa-vati' is a Sanskrit composite word, which means "one with plenty of water". Devi Saraswati is the mother of all four Vedas and goddess of music, arts , knowledge, wisdom, consciousness. Saraswati is the Shakti, the power and the consort of Brahma 'the creator. She is described as a beautiful fair Goddess with four arms, wearing white saree and seated on a white lotus. Her four arms represent the four aspects of human personality : manas (mind, sense), buddhi (intellect, reasoning), citta(i) (imagination, creativity), and ahamkāra (self consciousness, ego).Alternatively, these four arms also represent the Four Vedas. Because of these Saraswati Vandana' often begin and end Vedic lessons. Delegacies of Maa Sarasvatīare also found in Jainsm and in Buddhism. Regular reciting of Saraswati mantra improves mind, memory and concentration. Recitation and chanting of Saraswati Mantra can help students studies and a job seekers to clear their interview successfully. Stunents who are aspiring to go in for higher studies and research work can benefit tremendously from regular chanting (Japa) of Maa Saraswati Mantra.

Puja and Festival Celebration dedicated to Maa Sarasvatī

- Vasanta Panchami (Saraswati's birthday)
- SarasvatīPuja
- Navrathiri (Seven,Eight and Ninth days of Navaratri)
- Mondays, Panchami (5th Day of Lunar Calender)

(Note: Please check and verify exact dates of festival celebrations in Hindu calendars or Panchang)

***

MAA SARASVATĪ PUJA MANTRAS

"Performing this puja with devotion and faith can bestow proficiency, success, and peace of mind "

Invocation to Lord Ganesh

Vakra-Tunndda Maha-Kaaya Suurya-Kotti Samaprabha |
Nirvighnam Kuru Me Deva Sarva-Kaaryessu Sarvadaa ||

वक्रतुण्ड महाकाय सूर्यकोटि समप्रभ ।
निर्विघ्नं कुरु मे देव सर्वकार्येषु सर्वदा ॥

Salutations to Sri Ganesha : O Lord, Who has a Curved Trunk, Who has a Large Body, Whose aura is like light of crores of sun, Please make my entire work obstacle free, forever.

Chanting of this mantra helps to achieve wealth, wisdom, good luck, prosperity and success in all the endeavors.

Shanthi Mantra

Om Saha Naav (au)-Avatu |
Saha Nau Bhunaktu |
Saha Viiryam Karavaavahai |
Tejasvi Naav[au]Adhii tam-Astu Maa

Vidvissaavahai |
Om Shaantih: Shaantih: Shaantih: ||

ॐ सह नाववतु ।
सह नौ भुनक्तु ।
सह वीर्यं करवावहै ।
तेजस्वि नावधीतमस्तु मा विद्विषावहै ।
ॐ शान्तिः शान्तिः शान्तिः ॥

Om, May He protect us both together; may He nourish us both togethe.Together may we perform . May what has been Studied by us be vigorous and effective; .Om! Let there be peace in me! May peace be unto us, and may peace be unto all living beings.

This Shanti mantra, prayer for peace found in the krishna Yajurveda Taittiriya Upanishad (2.2.2).This mantra purifies the body and relieves it from the sufferings, diseases and discomforts.

Asana Puja

Om Prthvi Tvayaa Dhrtaa Lokaa
Devi Tvam Vissnnunaa Dhrtaa |
Tvam Ca Dhaaraya Maam Devi
Pavitram Kuru Ca-[A]asanam ||

ॐ पृथ्वि त्वया धृता लोका
देवि त्वं विष्णुना धृता ।
त्वं च धारय मां देवि
पवित्रं कुरु चासनम् ॥

Om, O Prithivi Devi /Bhoomi Devi, You are borne the entire world Please hold me O Devi, and make this seat of the worshipper Pure.

Deepa Puja

Shubham Karoti Kalyaannam-Aarogyam Dhana-Sampadaa |
Shatru-Buddhi-Vinaashaaya Diipa-Jyotir-Namostute ||

शुभं करोति कल्याणमारोग्यं धनसंपदा ।
शत्रुबुद्धिविनाशाय दीपज्योतिर्नमोऽस्तुते ॥

Salutations to the Light of the Lamp, Which Brings Auspiciousness, Health and Prosperity; Which Destroys Inimical Feelings

Gayatri Mantra for Pranayama

Om Bhuuh : Om Bhuvah: Om Svah:
Om Mahah :Om Janah : Om Tapah: Om Satyam
Om Tat-Savitur Varennyam Bhargo Devasya Dhiimahi
Dhiyo Yo Nah Pracodayaat |
Om Aapo Jyotii Rasoa Amrtam Brahma Bhuur Bhuvah: SvarOm ||

(Touch the ears three times and saying Om, Om , Om)

ॐ भूः ॐ भुवः ॐ स्वः

ॐ महः ॐ जनः ॐ तपः ॐ सत्यम्
ॐ तत्सवितुर्वरेण्यं भर्गो देवस्य धीमहि
धियो यो नः प्रचोदयात् ।
ॐ आपो ज्योती रसोऽमृतं ब्रह्म भूर्भुवः स्वरोम् ॥

Yajur Veda: Taittiriya Aranyaka

Om,I meditate on the Consciousness of the Physical Plane, Om, I meditate on the intercede Space, Om, I meditate on the Heaven, Consciousness of the beginning of the Divine Mind.(the meditation goes to subtler levels)

This strengthens our mind with concentration and gives immense peace to us.

SANKALPA MANTRA

For Saivas :

Mamo partha samastha duritha
kshaya dwara ,
Sri Parameshwara preethyartham
Sri Sarasvatīprasada sidhyartham
Asmaham Sakudumbanam
shemasya, dhairyasya, dhairya,
vijaya, ayur, arogya, ishwarya, abhiv-
rithyartham, Kalyana Prapyartham,
Sakala vasikaranartham
Mahaganaptim pujam karishye

For Vaishnavas:

Mamo partha samastha duritha

**kshaya dwara ,
Sri Narayana Preethyartham
Sri Sarasvatīprasada sidhyartham
Asmaham Sakudumbanam
shemasya, dhairyasya, dhairya,
vijaya, ayur, arogya, ishwarya, abhiv-
rithyartham, Kalyana Prapyartham,
Sakala vasikaranartham
Mahaganaptim pujam karishye**

Om For removing all problems and pains in life.For making Lord happy. For blessings of Goddess Parvathi. For getting my above wishes fulfilled.

The procedure of making a decision to perform the pooja for the welfare of all concerned.

Kalash(a) Puja

**Kalashasya mukhe Vishnu: kanTe
rudrassamaasrita:|
Mule tatra sthitho brahma madhye
matrugana: smruta: ||
kukshou thu saagara: sarve sapthadveepa
vasundhara: |
Rigvedoatha yajurveda: saama vedo
atharvavana: ||
angaischa sahita ssarve
kalashaambu samaasrita: |**

कलशस्य मुखे विष्णु: कण्ठे रुद्र: समाश्रित:|
मूले तस्य स्थितो ब्रह्मा मध्ये मातृगणा: स्थिता ||

कुक्षौ तु सागर: सर्वे सप्तद्वीपा वसुन्धरा |
ग्वेंदो यजुर्वेद: सामवेदो अथर्वण: ||
अङ्गैश्च सहितं सर्वे कलशाम्बु समाश्रिता: |

Kalash(a) is traditionally a copper pot. Fill it up with water and put two or three leaves of tulsi leaves or flower petals as well . Take few more couple of flower petals (or Tulsi leaves) dip it in the pot water and sprinkle it around the area you are seated . Then sprinkle the few drops of water if,other people seated around you .

Invite all the holy rivers like Ganga,yamuna, saraswati,narmada, godavari, sindhu,kaveri into this water pot . Invite all the gods ie Brahma, Vishnu, Shiva, Ganesh. (May come to me to bestow Peace and remove the Evil Influences)

Ghanta Puja

Aagama Artham Tu Devaanaam Gamana Artham Tu Rakssasaam |
Ghannttaa Ravam Karomya(ia)adau Devataa Ahvaana Laan chanam ||

आगमार्थं तु देवानां गमनार्थं तु रक्षसाम् ।
घण्टारवं करोम्यादौ देवताह्वान लाञ्छनम् ॥

For the purpose of inviting the Divine Forces and removing Evil Forces, I make the (Ghanta) Bell Sound.

Sarasvatī Dhyana Mantra

Om Saraswati Mayaa Drishtwa,
Veena Pustak Dharnim |
Hans Vahini Samayuktaa Maa
Vidya Daan Karotu Me Om ||

ॐ सरस्वती मया दृष्ट्वा, वीणा पुस्तक धारणीम् ।
हंस वाहिनी समायुक्ता मां विद्या दान करोतु में ॐ ।।

Mantra of Meditation.Ode to the Goddess to tremendously enhance focussing power and retention capacity of the mind.

(Note: You can chant this mantra 3 or 9 or 18 times to get more benefit)

Sarasvatī Beej(ah) Mantra

Om Aing Mahasaraswatyai Namah ||

ॐ ऐं महासरस्वत्यै नमः ||

This Mantra is chanted by devotees as a salutations to Maa Saraswati. Chanting this Beej(ah) mantra of Saraswati can increase the intelligence and the power of speech.

(Note: You can chant this mantra 3 or 9 or 18 times to get more benefit)

SarasvatīVidhya Mantra

Saraswati Namasthubhyam Varade
Kamarupini
Vidyarambham KarishyamiSiddhir

Bavathume Sadha

सरस्वति नमस्तुभ्यं वरदे कामरूपिणि ।
विद्यारम्भं करिष्यामि सिद्धिर्भवतु मे सदा ॥

Salutations to Devi Saraswati, Who is the giver of Blessings and fulfiller of Wishes, O Devi, when I begin my Studies, Please bestow on me the capacity of Right Understanding, always.

This mantra is recommended for students to chant before they start studying. Maa Saraswati blesses them with the power of memory and concentration.

(Note: You can chant this mantra 3 or 9 or 18 times to get more benefit)

Sarasvatī Gayathri Mantra

Om aen Vageeshwaryae
Vidmahe Vagwadeenyae
Dhimahe Tannah Saraswati Prachodayat

ॐ ऐन वाग्देव्यै च विद्महे कामराजाय धीमहि!
तन्नो देवी प्रचोदयात ॥

This mantra is chanted to seek success from Devi Sarasvatīin career and education.

Four Powerful mantras of Maa Sarasvatī that solve all your Prayer

Mantra For Intelligence

Shuklaam Brahmvichaar Saar
Paramaadyaam Jagadvyaapineem
Veennaa Pushtak Dhaarinneebhamay
Daam Jaad Yaapandhkaaraapahaam
Haste Sfatik Maalikaam Vidhateem
Paramaasane Sansthitaam
Vande Taam Parameshwareem Bhagwa-
teem Buddhi Pradaam Shaaradaam.

शुक्लां ब्रह्मविचारसारपरमांद्यां जगद्व्यापनीं
वीणा-पुस्तक-धारिणीमभयदां जाड्यांधकारपहाम्।
हस्ते स्फाटिक मालिकां विदधतीं पद्मासने संस्थिताम्
वन्दे तां परमेश्वरीं भगवतीं बुद्धिप्रदां शारदाम्।।

Mantra for Wealth and Knowledge to Gain Wisdom

Om Arham Mukha Kamal Vaasinee
Paapaatma Kshayam Kaari
Vad Vad Vaagwaadinee Saraswati
Aing Hreeng Namah Swaaha ||

ॐ अर्हं मुख कमल वासिनी पापात्म क्षयम् कारी
वद वद वाग्वादिनी सरस्वती ऐं ह्रीं नमः स्वाहा ||

Rig Veda Mantra for illumination

Maho Arnnah Sarasvatii Pra
Cetayati Ketunaa |
Dhiyo Vishvaa Vi Raajati

महो अर्णः सरस्वती प्र चेतयति केतुना ।
धियो विश्वा वि राजति ॥

Mantra for gaining knowledge

Vad Vad Vaagwaadinee Swaha ॥

वद वद वाग्वादिनी स्वाहा ॥

(Note: You can chant these mantras 3 or 9 or 18 times to get more benefit)

Sarasvatī Vandana

Ya Kundendu Tusharahara Dhavala Ya Shubhra Vastravrita
Ya Veena Varadanda Manditakara Ya Shveta Padmasana |
Ya Brahmachyuta Shankara Prabhritibihi Devaih: Sada Pujita
Sa Mam Pattu Saravatee Bhagavatee Ni:hshesha Jadyapaha ॥1 ॥

या कुन्देन्दुतुषारहारधवला या शुभ्रवस्त्रावृता
या वीणावरदण्डमण्डितकरा या श्वेतपद्मासना।
या ब्रह्माच्युत शंकरप्रभृतिभिर्देवैः सदा वन्दिता
सा मां पातु सरस्वती भगवती निःशेषजाड्यापहा॥१॥

Shuklam Brahmavichara Sara, Parmamadyam Jagadvyapineem

Veena Pustaka Dharineema Bhayadam Jadyandhakarapaham ।
Haste Sphatikamalikam Vidadhateem Padmasane Samsthitam
Vande Tam Parmeshvareem Bhagwateem Buddhipradam Sharadam ॥2॥

शुक्लां ब्रह्मविचार सार परमामाद्यां जगद्व्यापिनीं
वीणा-पुस्तक-धारिणीमभयदां जाड्यान्धकारापहाम्।
हस्ते स्फटिकमालिकां विदधतीं पद्मासने संस्थिताम्
वन्दे तां परमेश्वरीं भगवतीं बुद्धिप्रदां शारदाम्॥ २॥

Salutations to Devi Saraswati, Who is pure white like Jasmine, with the coolness of Moon, and whose pure white garland is like frosty dew drops; She is adorned in radiant white attire, on whose beautiful arm rests the veena, and whose throne is a white lotus. She is surrounded and respected by the Gods. O Goddess Saraswati, please protect me and remove my ignorance completely.

Sharada Bhujanga Prayathashtakam

Suvakshoja Kumbha Sudha Poorna Kumbhaam
Prasada Valambhaam Prapunya Valambaam |
Sadasyendu Bhimbhaam Sada Noshta Bhimbhaam
Bhaje Saradambhaam Ajasram

Madhambham ||

सुवक्षोजकुम्भां सुधापूर्णकुम्भां
प्रसादावलम्बां प्रपुण्यावलम्बाम् ।
सदास्येन्दुबिम्बां सदानोष्ठबिम्बां
भजे शारदाम्बामजस्रं मदम्बाम् ॥

Kadakshe Dayardhraam Kare
Gnana Mudhraam
Kalabhir Vinidhram
Kalapai :Subhadhraam |
Purasthreem Vinidhraam
Puras Thungabhadram
Bhaje Saradambhaam Ajasram
Madhambham ||

कटाक्षे दयार्द्रां करे ज्ञानमुद्रां
कलाभिर्विनिद्रां कलापैः सुभद्राम् ।
पुरस्त्रीं विनिद्रां पुरस्तुङ्गभद्रां
भजे शारदाम्बामजस्रं मदम्बाम् ॥

Lalaa Manga Phaalaam Lasad Gana Lolaam
Swabhakthaika Paalaam Yasa
Sree Kapolaam |
Kare Thwaksha Maalaam Kanath
Prathna Lolaam
Bhaje Saradambhaam Ajasram
Madhambham ||

ललामाङ्कफालां लसद्गानलोलां
स्वभक्तैकपालां यशःश्रीकपोलाम् ।

करे त्वक्षमालां कनत्प्रत्नलोलां
भजे शारदाम्बामजस्रं मदम्बाम् ॥

Su Seemantha Veneem Drusa Nirjit Thaineem
Ramath Keera Vaneem Namath Vajra Panim |
Sudha Mandha Rasyam Mudha Chinthya Veneem
Bhaje Saradambhaam Ajasram Madhambham ||

सुसीमन्तवेणीं दृशा निर्जितैणीं
रमत्कीरवाणीं नमद्वज्रपाणीम् ।
सुधामन्थरास्यां मुदा चिन्त्यवेणीं
भजे शारदाम्बामजस्रं मदम्बाम् ॥

Susantham Sudeham Druganthe Kachanthaam
Lasad Salla Thagee Manthama Chinthyam |
Smara Thapasai Sanga Poorvas Thitham Thaam
Bhaje Saradambhaam Ajasram Madhambham.

सुशान्तां सुदेहां दृगन्ते कचान्तां
लसत् सल्लताङ्गीमनन्तामचिन्त्याम् ।
स्मतां तापसैः सर्गपूर्वस्थितां तां
भजे शारदाम्बामजस्रं मदम्बाम् ॥

Kurange Thurange Mrugendre Khagendre
Maraale Madhebhe Mahokshae
Dhi Rodaam
Mahathyam Navamyam Sada
Saama Roopam
Bhaje Saradambhaam Ajasram
Madhambham.

कुरङ्गे तुरङ्गे मृगेन्द्रे खगेन्द्रे
मराले मदेभे महोक्षेऽधिरूढाम् ।
महत्यां नवम्यां सदा सामरूपां
भजे शारदाम्बामजस्रं मदम्बाम् ॥

Jwalath Kanthi Vahnim Jagan
Moha Naamgeem
Bhaje Maanasam Bhoja Subrantha
Brungeem |
Nija Stotra Sangeetha Nruthya
Prabhangeem
Bhaje Saradambhaam Ajasram
Madhambham ||

ज्वलत्कान्तिवह्निं जगन्मोहनाङ्गीं
भजन्मानसाम्भोजसुभ्रान्तभृङ्गीम् ।
निजस्तोत्रसङ्गीतनृत्यप्रभाङ्गी
भजे शारदाम्बामजस्रं मदम्बाम् ॥

Bhavambhoja Nethraja Sam Poojya Manam
Lasan Manda Hasa Prabha Vakthra
Chihnaam |

Chlath Chanchalodhara Tha Danga Karnam Bhaje Saradambhaam Ajasram Madhambham ||

भवाम्भोजनेत्राजसम्पूज्यमानां
लसन्मन्दहासप्रभावक्त्रचिह्नाम् ।
चलच्चञ्चलाचारुताटङ्ककर्णां
भजे शारदाम्बामजस्रं मदम्बाम् ॥

Sharada Bhujanga Prayathashtakam, which was composed by one of India's foremost spiritual saints, Sri Adi Shankaracharya, around 810 AD. He dedicated the Stotram to Goddess Saraswathi, set in eight hymns. Sharada is the goddess of the temple town of Sringeri. She is supposed to be an incarnation of Goddess Saraswathi. Adhi Shankara has established one of his Mutts in this town.

Sarasvatī AśhṭottaraSata Nāmāvali

ॐ सरस्वत्यै नमः।
Om Saraswatyai Namah।

ॐ महाभद्रायै नमः।
Om Mahabhadrayai Namah।

ॐ महामायायै नमः।
Om Mahamayayai Namah।

ॐ वरप्रदायै नमः।
Om Varapradayai Namah।

ॐ श्रीप्रदायै नमः।
Om Shripadayai Namah।

ॐ पद्मनिलयायै नमः।
Om Padmanilayayai Namah।

ॐ पद्माक्ष्यै नमः।
Om Padmakshyai Namah।

ॐ पद्मवक्त्राकायै नमः।
Om Padmavaktrakayai Namah।

ॐ शिवानुजायै नमः।
Om Shivanujayai Namah।

ॐ पुस्तकभृते नमः।
Om Pustakabhrite Namah।

ॐ ज्ञानमुद्रायै नमः।
Om Jnanamudrayai Namah।

ॐ रमायै नमः।
Om Ramayai Namah।

ॐ परायै नमः।
Om Parayai Namah।

ॐ कामरूपायै नमः।
Om Kamarupayai Namah।

ॐ महाविद्यायै नमः।
Om Mahavidyayai Namah।

ॐ महापातक नाशिन्यै नमः।
Om Mahapataka Nashinyai Namah।

ॐ महाश्रयायै नमः।
Om Mahashrayayai Namah।

ॐ मालिन्यै नमः।

Om Malinyai Namah।

ॐ महाभोगायै नमः।

Om Mahabhogayai Namah।

ॐ महाभुजायै नमः।

Om Mahabhujayai Namah।

ॐ महाभागायै नमः।

Om Mahabhagayai Namah।

ॐ महोत्साहायै नमः।

Om Mahotsahayai Namah।

ॐ दिव्याङ्गायै नमः।

Om Divyangayai Namah।

ॐ सुरवन्दितायै नमः।

Om Suravanditayai Namah।

ॐ महाकाल्यै नमः।

Om Mahakalyai Namah।

ॐ महापाशायै नमः।

Om Mahapashayai Namah।

ॐ महाकारायै नमः।

Om Mahakarayai Namah।

ॐ महाङ्कुशायै नमः।

Om Mahankushayai Namah।

ॐ पीतायै नमः।

Om Pitayai Namah।

ॐ विमलायै नमः।
Om Vimalayai Namah।

ॐ विश्वायै नमः।
Om Vishwayai Namah।

ॐ विद्युन्मालायै नमः।
Om Vidyunmalayai Namah।

ॐ वैष्णव्यै नमः।
Om Vaishnavyai Namah।

ॐ चन्द्रिकायै नमः।
Om Chandrikayai Namah।

ॐ चन्द्रवदनायै नमः।
Om Chandravadanayai Namah।

ॐ चन्द्रलेखाविभूषितायै नमः।
Om Chandralekhavibhushitayai Namah।

ॐ सावित्र्यै नमः।
Om Savitryai Namah।

ॐ सुरसायै नमः।
Om Surasayai Namah।

ॐ देव्यै नमः।
Om Devyai Namah।

ॐ दिव्यालङ्कारभूषितायै नमः।
Om Divyalankarabhushitayai Namah।

ॐ वाग्देव्यै नमः।
Om Vagdevyai Namah।

ॐ वसुधायै नमः।

Om Vasudhayai Namah।

ॐ तीव्रायै नमः।

Om Tivrayai Namah।

ॐ महाभद्रायै नमः।

Om Mahabhadrayai Namah।

ॐ महाबलायै नमः।

Om Mahabalayai Namah।

ॐ भोगदायै नमः।

Om Bhogadayai Namah।

ॐ भारत्यै नमः।

Om Bharatyai Namah।

ॐ भामायै नमः।

Om Bhamayai Namah।

ॐ गोविन्दायै नमः।

Om Govindayai Namah।

ॐ गोमत्यै नमः।

Om Gomatyai Namah।

ॐ शिवायै नमः।

Om Shivayai Namah।

ॐ जटिलायै नमः।

Om Jatilayai Namah।

ॐ विन्ध्यावासायै नमः।

Om Vindhyavasayai Namah।

ॐ विन्ध्याचलविराजितायै नमः।
Om Vindhyachalavirajitayai Namah।

ॐ चण्डिकायै नमः।
Om Chandikayai Namah।

ॐ वैष्णव्यै नमः।
Om Vaishnavyai Namah।

ॐ ब्राह्मयै नमः।
Om Brahmyai Namah।

ॐ ब्रह्मज्ञानैकसाधनायै नमः।
Om Brahmajnanaikasadhanayai Namah।

ॐ सौदामिन्यै नमः।
Om Saudaminyai Namah।

ॐ सुधामूर्त्यै नमः।
Om Sudhamurtyai Namah।

ॐ सुभद्रायै नमः।
Om Subhadrayai Namah।

ॐ सुरपूजितायै नमः।
Om Surapujitayai Namah।

ॐ सुवासिन्यै नमः।
Om Suvasinyai Namah।

ॐ सुनासायै नमः।
Om Sunasayai Namah।

ॐ विनिद्रायै नमः।
Om Vinidrayai Namah।

ॐ पद्मलोचनायै नमः।

Om Padmalochanayai Namah।

ॐ विद्यारूपायै नमः।

Om Vidyarupayai Namah।

ॐ विशालाक्ष्यै नमः।

Om Vishalakshyai Namah।

ॐ ब्रह्मजायायै नमः।

Om Brahmajayayai Namah।

ॐ महाफलायै नमः।

Om Mahaphalayai Namah।

ॐ त्रयीमूर्त्यै नमः।

Om Trayimurtyai Namah।

ॐ त्रिकालज्ञायै नमः।

Om Trikalajnayai Namah।

ॐ त्रिगुणायै नमः।

Om Trigunayai Namah।

ॐ शास्त्ररूपिण्यै नमः।

Om Shastrarupinyai Namah।

ॐ शुम्भासुरप्रमथिन्यै नमः।

Om Shumbhasurapramathinyai Namah।

ॐ शुभदायै नमः।

Om Shubhadayai Namah।

ॐ स्वरात्मिकायै नमः।

Om Swaratmikayai Namah।

ॐ रक्तबीजनिहन्त्र्यै नमः।
Om Raktabijanihantryai Namah।

ॐ चामुण्डायै नमः।
Om Chamundayai Namah।

ॐ अम्बिकायै नमः।
Om Ambikayai Namah।

ॐ मुण्डकायप्रहरणायै नमः।
Om Mundakayapraharanayai Namah।

ॐ धूम्रलोचनमर्दनायै नमः।
Om Dhumralochanamardanayai Namah।

ॐ सर्वदेवस्तुतायै नमः।
Om Sarvadevastutayai Namah।

ॐ सौम्यायै नमः।
Om Saumyayai Namah।

ॐ सुरासुर नमस्कृतायै नमः।
Om Surasura Namaskritayai Namah।

ॐ कालरात्र्यै नमः।
Om Kalaratryai Namah।

ॐ कलाधारायै नमः।
Om Kaladharayai Namah।

ॐ रूपसौभाग्यदायिन्यै नमः।
Om Rupasaubhagyadayinyai Namah।

ॐ वाग्देव्यै नमः।
Om Vagdevyai Namah।

ॐ वरारोहायै नमः।

Om Vararohayai Namah।

ॐ वाराह्यै नमः।

Om Varahyai Namah।

ॐ वारिजासनायै नमः।

Om Varijasanayai Namah।

ॐ चित्राम्बरायै नमः।

Om Chitrambarayai Namah।

ॐ चित्रगन्धायै नमः।

Om Chitragandhayai Namah।

ॐ चित्रमाल्यविभूषितायै नमः।

Om Chitramalyavibhushitayai Namah।

ॐ कान्तायै नमः।

Om Kantayai Namah।

ॐ कामप्रदायै नमः।

Om Kamapradayai Namah।

ॐ वन्द्यायै नमः।

Om Vandyayai Namah।

ॐ विद्याधरसुपूजितायै नमः।

Om Vidyadharasupujitayai Namah।

ॐ श्वेताननायै नमः।

Om Shwetananayai Namah।

ॐ नीलभुजायै नमः।

Om Nilabhujayai Namah।

ॐ चतुर्वर्गफलप्रदायै नमः।
Om Chaturvargaphalapradayai Namah।

ॐ चतुरानन साम्राज्यायै नमः।
Om Chaturanana Samrajyayai Namah।

ॐ रक्तमध्यायै नमः।
Om Raktamadhyayai Namah।

ॐ निरञ्जनायै नमः।
Om Niranjanayai Namah।

ॐ हंसासनायै नमः।
Om Hamsasanayai Namah।

ॐ नीलजङ्घायै नमः।
Om Nilajanghayai Namah।

ॐ ब्रह्मविष्णुशिवान्मिकायै नमः।
Om Brahmavishnushivatmikayai Namah।

Ashtottara Shatanamavali means collective hundred and eight names of God or Goddess. 108 has been considered a sacred number in Hinduism.We find many Ashtottara Shatanamavalis in Purana as well as in epics like Mahabharata. These names are composed by Rishis, devotees, divine beings etc.

One of the benefits of chanting this SarasvatīAśhṭottara Sata Nāmāvaḻi is to tremendously enhance focussing power and retention capacity of the mind.

Prayer

Om Sarve Bhavantu Sukhinah

Sarve Santu Nir-Aamayaah |
Sarve Bhadraanni Pashyantu
Maa Kashcid-Duhkha-Bhaag-Bhavet |
Om Shaantih Shaantih Shaantih ||

ॐ सर्वे भवन्तु सुखिनः
सर्वे सन्तु निरामयाः ।
सर्वे भद्राणि पश्यन्तु
मा कश्चिद्दुःखभाग्भवेत् ।
ॐ शान्तिः शान्तिः शान्तिः ॥

Om, May All be prosperous and happy. May All be Free from Illness.May All See what is Auspicious and spiritually uplifting. May Nobody suffer.Om Peace, Peace, Peace.

*****

NAVRATRI PUJA

(VIJAYADASAMI)

Navaratri is a major Hindu long festival celebrated in the October (autumn) by millions of Hindus throughout the world. The word Navaratri is derived from Sanskrit language. According to Sanskrit, 'Nava' means nine and 'Ratri' means night and therefore this festival is called 'Navaratri'. Navarathiri is pronounced in many ways such as Navrathiri, Nauratri, Navarathri, Navratan, Nauratan etc., irrespective of its calling it is multifaceted nine night, ten days long festival celebration during which nine forms of Hindu Goddess Shakthi (Devi). According to the Devi Mahatyam, nine forms of Devi (Nava Durga) are

Śailaputrī : The first manifestation of Durga is Goddess Shailputri. Sati, Daughter of the Himālayas, Wife of Lord Shiva.

Brahmachāriṇī : The second day of Navratri is dedicated to Goddess Brahmacharini.She is also known as 'Uma' and 'Tapacharini'. She provides knowledge and wisdom.

Chandraghaṇṭā : The third manifestation of Durga is Goddess Chandraghanta, one who bears the moon in her necklace. She is depicted as a fierce 10-armed Goddess, roaring in anger.

Kūṣmāṇḍa : On the fourth day of Navratri, Goddess Kushmanda, the creator of the universe is worshipped. According to the puranas she controls whole Solar system.

Skanda-Mātā : The fifth manifestation of Durga is Skandmata. The mother of Skanda, Kārttikeya, born out of her powers who is worshiped on the fifth day of the Navratri also known as Panchami.

Kātyāyanī : Goddess Parvati had taken the avatar of

Goddess Katyayani, the 6th form of NavaDurga.She is daughter of sage Kātyāyana, who incarnated to help the Devas. Ma Katyayani has three eyes and four hands. The left hand holds a weapon and the other a lotus. She rides on a lion.

Kālarātrī : The 7th form of NavaDurga is known as Goddess Kalaratri (black as night, destroyer of Kālī).She is considered to be the most ferocious avatar of NavaDurga and is known for destroying ignorance and removing darkness from the universe.

Mahāgaurī : Durga Asthami or the eight day of Navratri is dedicated to Goddess Mahagauri (the wife of Lord Shiva, doing great penance). As per the scriptures, Mahagauri worshiped as the four-armed deity who rides on a bull or a white elephant.

Siddhidātrī: Worshiped on the ninth day, Goddess Siddhidhatri is projected as a four-armed deity sitting calmly on a lotus. Siddhidatri Devi is worshipped by all Gods, Saints, Yogis, and all common devotees who want to attain the religious assent.Provider of mystic powers.

First, second and third days of Navaratri are devoted to Goddess Maa Durga (Maa: Mother), the deity of power and energy. Fourth, fifth and Sixth days of Navratri are committed to Goddess Maa Lakshmi, the Goddess of wealth and prosperity. Seventh, eighth and ninth days (Durgashtami, Mahanavami and Vijayadashami) belong to Goddess Saraswati the deity of wisdom and learning. The tenth day is celebrated as Dussehra. On this very day, the demon king Ravana (dummy) burnt to wipe off evil and bad spirits from earth.

There are different stories associated with the festival of 'Navarathiri .There are primarily two stories which form the basis of Purana and Epic. According to the Devi Mahamaya, it is believed that goddess Durga battled with the buffalo demon Mahishasura to restore peace and Justice (Dharma). Based on great epic Ramayana,it is the victory of lord Rama over the cruel and demonic Ravana, the one who kidnapped his wife, Sita. However, Navratri is celebrated by worshipping different goddesses and celebrating their victory.

Navratri puja is believed to bring prosperity and wealth to the home. Maa Durga blesses the family with Health, Wealth an Victory.

EASY STEPS TO DO NAVRATRI PUJA AT HOME

Step#1

Arrange your Puja Room. Clean and Place the deity properly. Establish the Kalash(ah). (*Read Puja Essentials from Section 1)*

Step# 2

Try wear nine different colours during the nine days of Navratri to get maximum benefit

Maa Durga Puja

- *Day 1: orange-hued clothes*
- *Day 2: white-coloured clothes*
- *Day 3: red-hued clothes*

Maa Lakshmi Puja

- *Day 4: Royal blue color.*
- *Day 5: yellow clothes*
- *Day 6: Green, the colour of growth and prosperity*

Maa Saraswati Puja

- *Day 7 White/Grey Color*
- *Day 8: Ppurple-coloured clothes*
- *Day 9 Peacock green*

Step# 3

Read – 'Basic Steps & Rules to do Puja or Worship' in section1

Step# 4

Chant Mantras from "Maa Durga Puja" for Navratri Days 1,2,3 &10)
Chant Mantras from "Maa Lakshmi Puja" for Navratri Days 4,5 &6)
Chant Mantras from "Maa Saraswati Puja" for Navratri Day 7,8,&9)

***

THANKS

I hope you found this book useful!
So start sacred mantra chanting regularly and remove all your obstacles in life!
Please do share your experience and suggestions as a review in Amazon's Kindle store to appreciate my efforts. It will motivate me to write more. Once again, thank you for downloading and reading this book.

ABOUT THE AUTHOR

Santhi Sivakumar

Mrs.Santhi Sivakumar, holds a Masters Degree in Financial Management (MBA). She is running a Media Consulting Company with her husband since 2005 in Chennai, India. She produced many Training Videos, Ad Films and Television Shows. She has special interests in Culinary, Spiritual, Health, Literature, Education and Stock Market. Her book "Biryani: The king of Indian Cuisine" is one of the hotselling books in Amazon's Kindle store.

Made in the USA
Las Vegas, NV
10 October 2024

96644505R00066